Grades 4–5

Teaching
by
Design
in
Elementary
Mathematics

Grades 4–5

Teaching
by
Design
in
Elementary
Mathematics

Melinda Leong | Jennifer Stepanek
Linda Griffin | Lisa Lavelle

A Joint Publication

CORWIN
A SAGE Company

education
northwest

For information:

Corwin
A SAGE Company
2455 Teller Road
Thousand Oaks, California 91320
(800) 233-9936
Fax: (800) 417-2466
www.corwin.com

SAGE Ltd.
1 Oliver's Yard
55 City Road
London EC1Y 1SP
United Kingdom

SAGE India Pvt. Ltd.
B 1/I 1 Mohan Cooperative Industrial Area
Mathura Road, New Delhi 110 044
India

SAGE Asia-Pacific Pte. Ltd.
33 Pekin Street #02-01
Far East Square
Singapore 048763

A catalog record of this book is available from the Library of Congress.

ISBN 978-1-4129-8703-5 (pbk.)

10 11 12 13 14 10 9 8 7 6 5 4 3 2 1

Acquisitions Editor:	Dan Alpert
Associate Editor:	Megan Bedell
Editorial Assistant:	Sarah Bartlett
Production Editor:	Cassandra Margaret Seibel
Copy Editor:	Gretchen Treadwell
Typesetter:	C&M Digitals (P) Ltd.
Proofreader:	Jenifer Kooiman
Indexer:	Will Ragsdale
Cover Designer:	Michael Dubowe
Permissions Editor:	Karen Ehrmann

Contents

Acknowledgments

We were privileged to have the support of many contributors throughout the process of developing this book.

In particular, we would like to thank the teachers at Riverview Elementary School—Leslie Carroll, Marla Ernst, Kristy Geddes, Beth Moore, Raylene Sell, Sheri Wardlaw—and Green Acres Elementary School—Jana Horne, Evan Kay, Chelsea Lewis, Danae Standfield, Julie Verbeck, and Leah Yeager—in Lebanon, Oregon. Their enthusiasm, dedication, and willingness to try new things were instrumental in creating the *Teaching by Design* materials. We are especially grateful to Marla Ernst and Lebanon Community Schools for supporting and facilitating our work with this terrific group of people.

We would also like to thank our colleagues for their careful review of the manuscript and their thoughtful feedback and suggestions. Joe Ediger, Bill Jackson, Mark Mitchell, Julie Peck, Neil Portnoy, and Nanci Schneider were very generous with their time and expertise. Liza Finkel, Claire Gates, and Kit Peixotto also reviewed early drafts and provided indispensible support to the writing team.

About the Authors

Melinda Leong has served as a Senior Program Advisor in the Mathematics Education Unit at Education Northwest since 2001, providing leadership in designing effective professional development in mathematics learning, teaching, and assessment. Before joining Education Northwest, she worked with the New York City Board of Education in District 2 as a teacher and director for 11 years at the K–8 level. She was the founder and director of the Manhattan Academy of Technology in New York, a middle school focused on integrating technology into a three-year comprehensive and rigorous academic program. She holds a BA in education and American studies from Tufts University, an MA in elementary education from Hunter College at the City University of New York, an MA in administration and supervision from City College at the City University of New York, and a graduate certificate in middle school mathematics from Portland State University.

Jennifer Stepanek is a writer, editor, and researcher with Education Northwest in Portland, Oregon. She is the lead author of *Leading Lesson Study: A Practical Guide for Teachers and Facilitators* (2007), published by Corwin Press. She has worked with lesson study teams at a variety of sites in the Northwest to explore how teachers in the United States are adapting the Japanese model to fit their contexts and needs. She has written and edited a number of articles on lesson study and is also the coauthor of *An Invitation to Lesson Study*, an electronic resource designed to help facilitators and other professional development providers introduce lesson study to others. Her previous projects include serving as the editor of *Northwest Teacher*, a math and science journal; and writing publications for the *It's Just Good Teaching* series, research-based monographs on mathematics and science teaching.

Linda Griffin is an Assistant Professor in the Graduate School of Education and Counseling at Lewis & Clark College in Portland, Oregon, where she serves as the director of the Early MAT Early Childhood/Elementary Program. From 2004 to 2010, she served as the director of the Mathematics Education Unit at Education Northwest. Her professional background includes fourteen years as a middle and high school mathematics teacher, as well as eight years working on National Science Foundation grant projects focused on teacher enhancement, gender equity, and parent involvement in the area of mathematics. She has extensive experience conducting staff development and presenting workshops at regional and national conferences and has taught university courses in mathematics, including mathematics content courses for preservice elementary teachers. She holds a BA in mathematics from the University of California at Davis, an MA in teaching and teacher education from the University of Arizona, and an EdD in educational leadership from Northern Arizona University.

Lisa Lavelle is Senior Curriculum Specialist in Mathematics at American Institutes for Research (AIR) where she is primarily involved in curriculum design and professional development for teachers. She also teaches math methods at Portland State University as an adjunct instructor. Prior to joining AIR, she served as Senior Program Advisor in the Mathematics Education Unit at Education Northwest, taught mathematics in both middle school and high school, served as a support teacher for elementary school mathematics, and worked with both preservice and inservice teachers in professional development. She earned her BA in psychology with emphasis in computer science from Yale University and at the same time completed the Teacher Preparation Program in secondary mathematics at Yale. She went on to earn her MA in professional studies, middle school mathematics, from George Washington University.

Introduction

What Is *Teaching by Design?*

Teaching by Design in Elementary Mathematics is a series of professional development guides that helps teachers create and share knowledge for teaching mathematics. This guide is one of three volumes in a set that focuses on topics within number and operations from kindergarten through Grade 5. Each volume in the series is organized in 14 professional development sessions in which teams of teachers learn, share, and plan together in a structured, collaborative environment.

Through participation in the carefully sequenced sessions in each guide, teachers build the specialized understanding of mathematics and pedagogy that supports effective instruction. The culmination of this professional learning process is the development of a *prototype lesson*, a mathematics lesson collaboratively designed by the team. In teaching this prototype lesson in one or more teachers' classrooms, the team can investigate its impact on student learning. The cycle of investigating, planning, teaching, observing, debriefing, and revising a lesson together contributes to a climate of continuous professional learning.

Expected Outcomes for *Teaching by Design in Elementary Mathematics*

1. Teachers will deepen their content knowledge of important mathematical concepts for the grade level they teach.

2. Teachers will increase their understanding of how students learn these mathematical ideas.

3. Teachers will use their knowledge to develop effective lessons and improve instruction.

4. Teachers will enhance their collaboration skills.

Mathematical Content Topics

Several sources were consulted to identify the mathematical focus for each volume in the *Teaching by Design* series. The content is aligned with the topics in number and operations identified by the National Council of Teachers of Mathematics (NCTM) in *Curriculum Focal Points for Prekindergarten Through Grade 8 Mathematics* (2006). The focal points help teachers to hone in on the most important topics, make connections between topics, and to provide students with an integrated understanding of mathematics. The mathematical content of *Teaching by Design* also matches content topics in number and operations found in the *Common Core State Standards* (National Governors Association Center for Best Practices & Council of Chief State School Officers, 2010).

Number and operations was selected as the content area for these materials because it is the cornerstone of mathematics education in Grades K–5. All mathematics is grounded in number, including algebra, geometry, measurement, and statistics (NCTM, 2000). This area of the curriculum is often considered to be the most simple and straightforward because it is the mathematics with which young children start their education. But learning about number and operations is in fact a complex process that has been a primary area of research in mathematics education (Fuson, 2003; Kilpatrick, Swafford, & Findell, 2001).

Model of Professional Development

One of the strengths of the *Teaching by Design in Elementary Mathematics* process is its alignment with the characteristics of effective professional development for teachers (Borasi & Fonzi, 2002; Corcoran, 1995; Garet, Porter, Desimone, Birman, & Yoon, 2001; Hawley & Valli, 1999; Darling-Hammond, Wei, Andree, Richardson, & Orphanos, 2009; Wilson & Berne, 1999). Specifically, effective learning experiences for teachers include the following characteristics:

- Opportunities for collaboration
- Ongoing activities
- Focus on content
- Teacher-driven and classroom-based methods
- Active and hands-on activities
- Focus on student learning

The *Teaching by Design* approach has been developed with these characteristics in mind to preserve this connection to high-quality professional development.

Teachers who are implementing any model for collaborative professional development can use *Teaching by Design*. Figure 1 provides a list describing some of these models and their features. Teacher teams that have already established one of these models for ongoing, job-embedded professional development will find that *Teaching by Design* is easily implemented within any of these models.

Teachers familiar with lesson study will recognize many of its features in the *Teaching by Design* materials (Fernandez & Chokshi, 2002; Lewis, 2002; Stigler & Hiebert, 1999; Yoshida, 1999). The sessions in each volume have been structured to provide support for the powerful practices of lesson study within any collaborative professional development model. Some of the practices from lesson study that will be evident in the *Teaching by Design* volumes include the following activities:

- Analyzing teaching materials
- Focusing on important content
- Establishing precise and connected lesson goals
- Developing well-planned lessons
- Observing student learning
- Analyzing student understanding

Teacher teams that have not previously engaged in one of these professional development models will still be able to successfully implement *Teaching by Design*. An informal group of grade-level teaching partners can use the materials provided as a way to take a first step toward establishing one of these professional development models. The resources section includes some recommended readings about each model that will assist groups that want to know more about them.

Figure 1 Models of Professional Development

Critical friends groups (CFG)	A group of teachers work together to examine and change their classroom practice guided by established group processes and protocols.
	Typical features: • A CFG coach guides the teachers' work. • The team uses CFG protocols to structure conversations about curriculum, student work, or relevant readings.
Lesson study	Teachers collaborate to develop a lesson plan, teach and observe the lesson to collect data on student learning, and use their observations to refine their lesson.
	Typical features: • Lesson study teams are self-directed and democratic, but may work with a facilitator and outside advisors. • The team has established protocols for designing, observing, debriefing, and revising collaboratively designed lessons.
Mathematics coaching	A specialist works with teachers one-on-one to examine and improve classroom practice and to improve pedagogical content knowledge.
	Typical features: • The mathematics coach works with individual teachers or grade-level teams of teachers. • The coach and teachers commonly observe each other teaching a lesson or coteach lessons.
Professional learning teams	Small groups of teachers work together to improve instruction and student learning.
	Typical features: • Members of the group share leadership of the group. • The team engages in reading and discussion on topics of professional interest to the group.

Collaborating to Design a Prototype Lesson

Why Design?

The term *design* generally refers to the creation of a product in an artistic or highly skilled manner, and it is usually associated with the applied arts, engineering, and architecture. In these contexts, good design means that the product fits the needs of the people who will use it and the context in which it will be used.

One of the more specific definitions of design is the process of preparing a detailed and deliberate plan for accomplishing something (Merriam-Webster, 1993). This definition is the essence of *Teaching by Design*. It is a way to describe teachers' work that focuses on planning well-designed lessons that fit the needs of their students.

Some of the general practices of design have parallels with teaching, and include the following practices:

• Identifying and framing problems and needs
• Working collaboratively

- Gathering and analyzing information
- Determining performance criteria for successful solutions
- Generating alternative solutions and building prototypes
- Evaluating and selecting appropriate solutions
- Implementing choices
- Evaluating outcomes

> "A teacher ideally conceived is a designer who helps learners design themselves."
>
> —David Perkins, *Knowledge as Design*

When architects or mechanical designers work on a project, they almost always collaborate with other professionals. Designing a building, a computer, or a refrigerator is complicated work and requires the best thinking of a team of experts. Similarly, well-designed lessons are often the product of several teachers working together to think deeply about the goals and strategize the best ways to help students achieve them.

In Sessions 2 through 11 of *Teaching by Design*, you will discuss and explore aspects of mathematics teaching and learning that will prepare you for Session 12, in which you will work together as a design team to develop a well-planned lesson. After the lesson has been taught in one or more classes, in Sessions 13 and 14 you will discuss the lesson results, then revise and improve the lesson. While the focus is on a single lesson designed by the group, the learning gained from the collaborative process will influence the many other lessons you plan individually.

Why Prototype Lessons?

In product design, a prototype is the original form of the product that serves as the basis or standard for other versions of that product. Through the *Teaching by Design* process, teachers will collaborate to design a *prototype* lesson. This lesson is the context through which teachers explore their ideas and questions about how students learn challenging mathematical concepts. As they design the prototype lesson together, teachers explore how to sequence learning experiences that engage students with important mathematics while strengthening students' problem-solving abilities. For designers, the implementation of a prototype provides information to enhance future products. Likewise, the implementation of the prototype lesson provides teaching teams with insights about teaching and learning that can be applied to the development and delivery of future lessons.

The prototype lesson provides an opportunity to incorporate the mathematical and pedagogical knowledge teachers have gained through the *Teaching by Design* sequence. The resulting lesson plan is more detailed than a typical lesson plan and represents teachers' collective ideas about helping students understand important mathematical ideas. In addition to laying out the learning activities and the sequence of instruction, the plan for the prototype lesson includes background information about the instructional decisions that have been made, goals for student learning, carefully worded questions and prompts, anticipated student responses and teacher supports, and points of evaluation. Including all these elements in the lesson plan facilitates the observation, debriefing, and revision of the lesson. It also serves as a record of the professional learning for this team while they are engaged in these professional development sessions.

The prototype lesson offers teachers a perfect opportunity to apply their knowledge and understanding of the following areas:

- *Mathematics content,* including their understanding of how the mathematical concepts are interconnected
- *Students' prior knowledge,* including what students have learned in previous lessons and what they have learned in prior grade levels or through experiences outside the classroom
- *Learning progressions,* including ideas of how students develop increasingly sophisticated strategies, big ideas, and models

Overview of the Sessions

The materials are organized into a series of 14 work sessions, each approximately 90 minutes long.

Session 1   Getting Started
Session 2   Learning Landscape
Session 3   Addition and Subtraction With Like and Related Fractions
Session 4   Understanding Equivalent Fractions
Session 5   Problem Solving With Rational Numbers
Session 6   Decimal and Fraction Relationships
Session 7   Comparing and Ordering Decimals and Fractions
Session 8   Mathematical Models: Adding and Subtracting Fractions
Session 9   Mathematical Games: Adding and Subtracting Fractions and Decimals
Session 10   Understanding Standard Procedures
Session 11   Instruction to Support Fluency With Standard Procedures
Session 12   Designing the Prototype Lesson
Session 13   Discussing Results
Session 14   Reflecting On and Revising the Prototype Lesson

Sessions 1 and 2 establish a context for the work. In Session 1, teams will establish group norms and explore design principles. In Session 2, teachers will begin to develop components of a learning landscape for number and operations in fourth and fifth grades.

Sessions 3 through 11 focus on how children learn specific mathematical topics. The activities include opportunities to do mathematics problems, to examine how students learn, and to analyze and discuss student work. Some of the sessions include activities that focus on how the ideas from that session can be used to inform instruction.

Between sessions, teachers will engage in two types of activities. Student Connections activities are opportunities for teachers to observe student learning and collect student work. Investigating Instructional Materials activities are opportunities to analyze teaching resources. These activities are integral to subsequent sessions because they are used to help illustrate important mathematical and pedagogical ideas and allow teachers to apply their learning to their practice.

During Session 11, the team begins work on the prototype lesson. The process of designing the lesson may take more than one meeting to complete. When the lesson is ready, one or more team members implement the lesson with their students. Session 13 should occur after the teaching of the lesson and is structured to provide teachers with an opportunity to discuss what happened and to analyze evidence of student learning. Depending on how many teachers implement the lesson, some teams will need additional time for this discussion. Session 14 gives teachers the opportunity to revise the lesson, reflect on the professional development process, and identify next steps.

Many times throughout *Teaching by Design,* you will be directed to write in your journal. It will be helpful to organize your journal into three sections: (1) Activities, (2) Student Connections, and (3) Lesson Design Notes. We suggest using either a binder with tabs or a composition book or spiral notebook with tabbed sections in which you take notes and staple handouts.

Facilitating

Each of the sessions is designed to be facilitated by one person. The facilitator can be a coach or team leader, or the facilitation role can rotate within the group. When team members take turns serving in this role, all of the teachers receive an opportunity to develop their leadership skills. In either case, the facilitator should take responsibility for previewing the session content and making sure that all the materials are prepared. During the session, the facilitator should also serve as the timekeeper and maintain the pace of the session.

Each session includes Facilitator Notes, outlining the specific responsibilities for that session. The notes include additional information the facilitator can use to support the work of the team. One of the key responsibilities during facilitation is helping to maintain the group norms that the team identifies in the first session. It is usually helpful for the team to revisit the list of group norms periodically to make sure they are adhering to the norms and to identify any additions or modifications to the list.

Another key responsibility for the facilitator is listening actively to the group's conversations throughout the session. The facilitator will help monitor the discussions and activities to ensure that all team members have an opportunity to participate, share their knowledge, and learn. The facilitator can also help get the discussions started with an initial observation or question if there is a lag in the conversation.

If a leader or coach will serve as the facilitator, keep in mind that the team is intended to be self-directed. All members of the team are responsible for making decisions, contributing equally to the work, and supporting their colleagues' professional learning. The resources listed at the end of this section provide for more information on the skills and responsibilities of facilitators in different types of professional learning teams.

Finding Time for Collaboration

Teaching by Design in Elementary Mathematics is intended to guide teams of teachers through a process of collaborative investigation that will deepen their knowledge for teaching mathematics. To engage in *Teaching by Design* sessions, teachers will need time to meet together. Ideally, each group will meet regularly and frequently. Having weekly or biweekly meetings keeps the momentum going while also allowing time for collecting student data between the sessions.

When opportunities for teacher collaboration are a regular part of the school schedule, finding time should not be an issue. However, even if collaboration time is not part of the existing schedule, teams can find other ways to meet. For example, team meetings can be held outside regular school hours before or after school. Teams may find that they have occasional opportunities to work for extended sessions on early-release days or on days scheduled for professional development. If this is the case, groups can complete more than one 90-minute session in that setting and collect student data to share at a subsequent meeting.

There are a number of excellent resources that specifically address the issues associated with finding time within the school schedule for school-based professional development and teacher collaboration time. Figure 2 illustrates the strategies schools have used to create more time for teachers to work together.

Figure 2   Strategies for Creating Time for Collaboration

Adjusting the School Schedule
Early Release/Late Start Four days a week, the school schedule is extended by several minutes. One day a week, students come to school one hour late or go home one hour early. A variation on this schedule is to have teachers come to school 30 minutes early, with students arriving 30 minutes late; a similar strategy can also be used at the end of the day. (An early release/late start schedule does not have to be used on a weekly basis but can be spread out over the course of several weeks.)
Professional Development Days The daily school schedule is extended by several minutes in order to release students for a full day once a month or every six weeks.
Prep Time Teachers in each grade level or each department have a common prep time that can be used weekly (or as needed) to work together.
Covering Classes
Specialist Days Each day of the week, students from one grade level spend most of the day with specialists, in the computer lab, and in the library.
Service Learning For one half-day each week, students spend their time conducting service learning or community projects.
Paraprofessionals/Administrators/Parents/Volunteers Teachers' classes are taken over for one hour each week.
Teaming Teacher teams pair up and take each other's classes for one hour each week. For example, each second-grade teacher takes one class of first graders so that the first-grade teachers can meet together.
Substitute Teachers Substitutes are hired to rotate through the classes one day every other week.
Reallocating Existing Time
Staff Meetings Weekly staff meetings are cut back to once or twice a month and replaced with grade-level or department meetings.
Adjusting Planning Time Teachers' daily planning time is used for collaborative work one day a week. The number of minutes that teachers are expected to stay after school can be cut back by 10 minutes on four days during the week in order to create an extra 40 minutes for meeting together on one afternoon.
Professional Development/Inservice Days Teachers are excused from staff development days to compensate for weekly meetings outside school hours.

References

Borasi, R., & Fonzi, J. (2002). *Professional development that supports school mathematics reform* (Vol. 3). Arlington, VA: National Science Foundation.

Corcoran, T. B. (1995). *Helping teachers teach well: Transforming professional development* (CPRE Policy Brief No. RB–16). New Brunswick, NJ: Rutgers, State University of New Jersey, Consortium for Policy Research in Education.

Darling-Hammond, L., Wei, R. C., Andree, A., Richardson, N., & Orphanos, S. (2009). *Professional learning in the learning profession: A status report on teacher development in the United States and abroad.* Oxford, OH: National Staff Development Council.

Design. (1993). *Merriam-Webster's collegiate dictionary* (10th ed.). Springfield, MA: Merriam-Webster.

Fernandez, C., & Chokshi, S. (2002). A practical guide to translating lesson study for a U.S. setting. *Phi Delta Kappan, 84*(2), 128–134.

Fuson, K. C. (2003). Developing mathematical power in whole number operations. In J. Kilpatrick, W. G. Martin, & D. Schifter (Eds.), *A research companion to Principles and Standards for School Mathematics* (pp. 68–94). Reston, VA: National Council of Teachers of Mathematics.

Garet, M. S., Porter, A. C., Desimone, L., Birman, B. F., & Yoon, K. S. (2001). What makes professional development effective? Results from a national sample of teachers. *American Educational Research Journal, 38*(4), 915–945.

Hawley, W. D., & Valli, L. (1999). The essentials of effective professional development: A new consensus. In L. Darling-Hammond & G. Sykes (Eds.), *Teaching as the learning profession: Handbook of policy and practice* (pp. 127–150). San Francisco: Jossey-Bass.

Kilpatrick, J., Swafford, J., & Findell, B. (Eds.). (2001). *Adding it up: Helping children learn mathematics.* Washington, DC: National Academies Press.

Lewis, C. (2002). *Lesson study: A handbook of teacher-led instructional change.* Philadelphia: Research for Better Schools.

National Council of Teachers of Mathematics (2000). *Principles and standards for school mathematics.* Arlington, VA: Author.

National Council of Teachers of Mathematics. (2006). *Curriculum focal points for prekindergarten through grade 8 mathematics: A quest for coherence.* Reston, VA: Author.

National Governors Association Center for Best Practices, & Council of Chief State School Officers. (2010). *Common Core State Standards: Mathematics.* Retrieved from http://www.corestandards.org/the-standards/mathematics/

Stigler, J. W., & Hiebert, J. (1999). *The teaching gap: Best ideas from the world's teachers for improving education in the classroom.* New York: Free Press.

Wilson, S. M., & Berne, J. (1999). Teacher learning and the acquisition of professional knowledge: An examination of research on contemporary professional development. In A. Iran-Nejad & P. D. Pearson (Eds.), *Review of research in education* (Vol. 24, pp. 173–209). Washington, DC: American Educational Research Association.

Yoshida, M. (1999, April). *Lesson study [jugyokenkyu] in elementary school mathematics in Japan: A case study.* Paper presented at the annual meeting of the American Educational Research Association, Montreal, Canada.

Additional Resources

Critical Friends Groups

National School Reform Faculty
http://www.nsrfharmony.org/faq.html#1

Coalition of Essential Schools Northwest
http://www.cesnorthwest.org/cfg.php

Allen, D., & Blythe, T. (2004). *A facilitator's book of questions: Resources for looking together at student and teacher work.* New York: Teachers College Press.

Lesson Study

Lesson Study Group at Mills College
http://www.lessonresearch.net/

Lesson Study Northwest Regional Educational Laboratory, Center for Classroom Teaching and Learning
http://educationnorthwest.org/service/235

Lewis, C. (2002). *Lesson study: A handbook of teacher-led instructional change.* Philadelphia: Research for Better Schools.

Stepanek, J., Appel, G., Leong, M., Mangan, M. T., & Mitchell, M. (2007). *Leading lesson study: A practical guide for teachers and facilitators.* Thousand Oaks, CA: Corwin.

Mathematics Coaches

Examining the Role of a Math Content Coach Eye on Education
http://www.eyeoneducation.com/Excerpts/7093-8%20Math%20Coaching%20Chapter%201.pdf

Pedagogical Content Coaching Silicon Valley Mathematics Initiative
http://www.noycefdn.org/documents/math/pedagogicalcontentcoaching.pdf

West, L., & Staub, F. C. (2003). *Content-focused coaching: Transforming mathematics lessons.* Portsmouth, NH: Heinemann.

Professional Learning Teams

Hord, S. M. (1997). Professional Learning Communities: What Are They and Why Are They Important? *Issues . . . About Change, 6*(1). Retrieved from www.sedl.org/change/issues/issues61.html

Sather, S. E. (2005). *Improving instruction through professional learning teams: A guide for school leaders.* Portland, OR: Northwest Regional Educational Laboratory. Retrieved from http://educationnorthwest.org/catalog/improving-instruction-through-professional-learning-teams-guide-school-leaders

Professional Learning Teams (PLTs) to Improve Student Achievement Education Northwest
http://educationnorthwest.org/service/295

Session **1**

Getting Started

Overview

What can we do to create the conditions that enhance professional learning?

Description

The need for collaborative professional learning is well established, but forming a group is only the first step. Collaboration can be challenging, so laying the groundwork for an effective and worthwhile experience is key. In this session, you will initiate *Teaching by Design* by establishing a common understanding of the process, group norms, and shared goals.

Key Ideas

- Some of the general practices of design have parallels with teaching.
- Well-designed lessons are often the product of several teachers working together to think deeply about their goals and strategize the best ways to help students achieve them.
- Establishing group norms helps a team to operate productively.
- Groups function best when they have a common understanding of their goals and outcomes.

Outline of Activities

- 1.1 What Is *Teaching by Design?*   (15 minutes)
- 1.2 To the Finish Line   (25 minutes)
- 1.3 *Teaching by Design* Themes   (20 minutes)
- 1.4 Setting Group Norms   (15 minutes)
- 1.5 Group Outcomes and Personal Goals   (10 minutes)
- 1.6 Before the Next Session   (5 minutes)

What to Bring

- A journal (see the description and suggestions in the Introduction) and writing instruments (bring these to every session)

To Complete Before Session 2

- Lesson Design Notes (Handout 1.3)

Facilitator Notes   Session 1

Getting Started

Before the session, please review the more detailed facilitator guidelines in the Introduction. As the facilitator, it is generally your job to keep the conversation flowing and watch the clock. Use your judgment to decide when it's appropriate to extend a session for good conversation or when it's time to move on to the next activity. Remember to keep the group norms posted and revise them, as a group, as necessary.

Before the Session

- Make copies of the following handouts for each team member:
  - ☐ 1.1 Design Practices
  - ☐ 1.2A To the Finish Line
  - ☐ 1.2B To the Finish Line Game Board
  - ☐ 1.2C To the Finish Line Playing Cards
  - ☐ 1.3 Lesson Design Notes
- Gather the following materials to be used in this session:
  - ☐ Chart paper
  - ☐ Markers
  - ☐ Counters or chips
  - ☐ Prepared sets of game cards (Handout 1.2C) on card stock (see Handout 1.2A)
- Remind team members to bring the following items:
  - ☐ Journal (see the description and suggestions in the Introduction)
  - ☐ Writing instruments

During the Session

- Activity 1.1: facilitate discussion; facilitate partnering and sharing, if necessary; serve as timekeeper.
- Activity 1.2: facilitate grouping, if necessary; serve as timekeeper.
- Activity 1.3: facilitate discussion.
- Activity 1.4: lead development of group norms; serve as recorder.

After the Session

- Pass the group norms on to the next facilitator.

Activity 1.1 What Is *Teaching by Design?*

15 minutes   Handout 1.1 Design Practices

Teaching by Design in Elementary Mathematics is a guide for professional development that helps teachers improve their knowledge for teaching mathematics. By engaging in the *Teaching by Design* process as a team, you will build a better understanding of mathematics and student learning.

We purposefully chose to link the terms *teaching* and *design* to describe this professional development experience. As noted in the Introduction, the term *design* is often associated with the applied arts, engineering, and architecture to describe the creation of a product in an artistic or highly skilled manner. Design in these contexts involves establishing goodness of fit between a product, the people who will use it, and the context in which it will be used. *Teaching by Design* is a way to describe teachers' work that focuses on planning deliberate and purposeful lessons that fit the needs of their students.

Discuss the following list of design practices with a partner. Consider how these practices might be applied to planning and teaching a lesson. Handout 1.1 provides this list in a table that can be used to record your ideas.

- Identifying and framing problems and needs
- Working collaboratively
- Gathering and analyzing information
- Determining performance criteria for successful solutions
- Generating alternative solutions and building prototypes
- Evaluating and selecting appropriate solutions
- Implementing choices
- Evaluating outcomes

Share what you and your partner listed with the whole group. In what ways does teaching include some of these design principles? Which ones have the strongest parallels to lesson design?

Activity 1.2 To the Finish Line

25 minutes   Handout 1.2A To the Finish Line
                                          Handout 1.2B To the Finish Line Game Board
                                          Handout 1.2C To the Finish Line Playing Cards
                                                              Counters or chips

Throughout the *Teaching by Design* experience, you will have the chance to engage in student activities that can be used in your classroom. Participating in these activities and analyzing their instructional benefits is intended to stimulate discussion of a range of teaching and learning issues. **Read** the description of the To the Finish Line game on Handout 1.2A.

Play the game with a group of two to four players for 15 minutes.

Discuss the following questions:

- What thinking processes did you use while engaging in this activity?
- What fraction and decimal concepts were reinforced while engaging in this activity?
- Is this mathematical activity similar to any activities you use in your classroom? Describe the related activities.
- Is this mathematical activity appropriate for your students? If not, what adaptations could you make so it would be appropriate for your students?

Activity 1.3 *Teaching by Design* Themes

20 minutes   Handout 1.3 Lesson Design Notes

As you and your team engage in the *Teaching by Design* sessions, you will discuss and explore many aspects of mathematics teaching and learning that will prepare you to work together to collaboratively plan a mathematics lesson. Each session will include opportunities for you to reflect on three key themes related to teaching and learning.

Read the following quotation about teaching and think about how it relates to your own experiences.

> To teach math, you need to know three things. You need to know where you are now (in terms of the knowledge children in your classroom have available to build upon). You need to know where you want to go (in terms of the knowledge you want all children in your classroom to acquire during the school year). Finally, you need to know what is the best way to get there (in terms of the learning opportunities you will provide to enable all children in your class to achieve your stated objectives). Although this sounds simple, each of these points is just the tip of an iceberg. Each raises a question (e.g., Where are we now?) that I have come to believe is crucial for the design of effective mathematics instruction. Each also points to a body of knowledge (the iceberg) to which teachers must have access in order to answer that question . . .
>
> By asking this set of questions every time I sat down to design a math lesson for young children, I was able to push my thinking further and, over time, construct better answers and better lessons. If each math teacher asks this set of questions on a regular basis, each will be able to construct his or her own set of answers for the questions, enrich our knowledge base, and improve mathematics teaching and learning for at least one group of children.
>
> Sharon Griffin,
> *How Students Learn* (2005, p. 257–258)

Discuss the three questions described in the quotation and apply them to your classroom.

Record your ideas on Handout 1.3 Lesson Design Notes.

- Where are you now?
  - What knowledge do your students currently have about fractions and decimals? What are they able to do and what do they understand?
  - Which of your students have greater needs than others? Describe the range of understanding that your students are currently demonstrating.
  - How can you find out more about each student's mathematical understanding?

- Where do you want to go?
  - What are your long-term goals for students?
  - What do you want your students to know and understand by the end of fourth or fifth grade?
  - What attitudes and beliefs about mathematics do you want your students to develop?

- What is the best way to get there?
  - What routines do you use that support student learning?
  - How do you identify and choose instructional approaches?
  - How do you use your knowledge of your students' current levels of understanding to inform your instructional decisions?
  - How do you scaffold your lessons to provide support for students who need extra help and challenge those students who finish quickly?

You will continue to add new ideas and questions to the Lesson Design Notes in future sessions. Staple or tape Handout 1.3 into your journal and set up a section with room for additional notes. This will help you capture all of your lesson design ideas in one place.

Activity 1.4 Setting Group Norms

15 minutes

Collaboration can be challenging at times, even in a group of willing and committed partners. Laying the groundwork for an effective and worthwhile experience is key to managing any bumps in the road.

Consider the following questions and **write** your answers in your journal. Treat this like a brainstorming activity. Try to get as many ideas on paper as possible.

- What expectations do you have for how the group will work together?

- What conditions get in the way of learning and sharing?

- What group features help you to feel a sense of belonging and support?

Before you share your list with the group and develop group norms, read the following ideas about effective group processes (Bray, Lee, Smith, & Yorks, 2000; Collay, Dunlap, Enloe, & Gagnon, 1998; Dufour & Eaker, 1998; Preskill & Torres, 1999). Reading this list might prompt new ideas that you would like to add to your journal, so feel free to add to or edit your list based on the following ideas.

- *Groups work well when communication is open and honest.* Team members must feel that they are able to share their ideas and opinions without inspiring defensiveness or reprisals. It will be difficult for members to learn from each other if they cannot be honest. Although the ability to share their views openly and honestly is important, members will be unlikely to do so if they fear their contributions will be ignored or belittled. The balance between honesty and trust may not be easy to establish and maintain at first, but it is crucial to the team's work.

- *Groups work well when members both challenge and support each other.* Team members do this by asking questions, building on each other's ideas, and respectfully disagreeing. They are expected to ask for clarification, explain their reasoning, and provide evidence to back up their assertions.

- *Groups work well when methods for resolving conflict are established and agreed upon.* No team should begin its work with the assumption that it will be easy to work together. Members must agree to listen and focus on the problem rather than on the people involved, give the process adequate time, and try to see the issue from another person's perspective.

- *Groups work well when mistakes are viewed as opportunities.* It is difficult to try new things or to take risks if you fear the consequences. It may be helpful to keep in mind that mistakes are fruitful sources of learning—so, in many ways, the more the better.

- *Groups work well when all members are held accountable for their actions.* Part of engaging in collaborative learning is making a commitment to the other team members. All must agree to fulfill their specific responsibilities, to share the work as equally as possible, and to support each other and maintain productive and respectful interactions.

Share your list with the group. The facilitator will keep a running list on chart paper as each person takes turns sharing. Keep going around the room until all ideas are represented on the paper. **Discuss** and **refine** the list so that it reflects the consensus of the group.

Maintaining Group Norms

This list of group norms will serve as a charter for your team. The final list should be posted each time the group meets or it can be transferred to a handout that group members keep in their journals.

Remember that establishing group norms is only the first step. You will need to continually monitor your own participation and hold your colleagues to the norms. Do not wait until a problem arises to review the list and reflect on your collaborative practices.

Activity 1.5 Group Outcomes and Personal Goals

10 minutes

Teaching by Design in Elementary Mathematics has the following expected outcomes.

Expected Outcomes for *Teaching by Design*

1. Teachers will deepen their content knowledge of important mathematical concepts for the grade level they teach.
2. Teachers will increase their understanding of how students learn these mathematical ideas.
3. Teachers will use their knowledge to develop effective lessons and improve instruction.
4. Teachers will enhance their collaboration skills.

Discuss what each outcome means to you. Do these outcomes match your own expectations for this professional development process? What additional goals do you have for the group?

Write your answers to some of the following questions in your journal:

- How do you expect this professional development process to impact your teaching?
- In what ways do you think this process will impact your relationships with your colleagues in this group?
- What personal goals do you have for your work with *Teaching by Design?*

Activity 1.6 Before the Next Session

5 minutes

Write additional questions and ideas on your Lesson Design Notes. As you work with your students between now and the next sessions, find out more about their mathematical understanding and add this data under "Where are you now?"

Read the Introduction to *Teaching by Design in Elementary Mathematics* if you have not done so already. This will give you a broader sense of the intent of this type of professional development as well as some tips for facilitating your time together. Consider how your personal goals are connected to the *Teaching by Design* process.

References and Resources

Bray, J. N., Lee, J., Smith, L. L., & Yorks, L. (2000). *Collaborative inquiry in practice: Action, reflection, and making meaning.* Thousand Oaks, CA: Sage.

Collay, M., Dunlap, D., Enloe, W., & Gagnon, G. W., Jr. (1998). *Learning circles: Creating conditions for professional development.* Thousand Oaks, CA: Corwin.

Dufour, R., & Eaker, R. (1998). *Professional learning communities at work: Best practices for enhancing student achievement.* Bloomington, IN: National Educational Service.

Griffin, S. (2005). Fostering the development of whole number sense: Teaching mathematics in the primary grades. In M. S. Donovan & J. D. Bransford (Eds.), *How students learn: Mathematics in the classroom* (pp. 257–308). Washington, DC: National Academies Press.

Preskill, H., & Torres, R. T. (1999). *Evaluative inquiry for learning in organizations.* New York: Doubleday.

Handout 1.1
Design Practices

Design Practices in Applied Arts, Engineering, and Architecture	Application of the Practice to Lesson Planning and Lesson Delivery
Identifying and framing problems and needs	
Working collaboratively	
Gathering and analyzing information	
Determining performance criteria for successful solutions	
Generating alternative solutions and building prototypes	
Evaluating and selecting appropriate solutions	
Implementing choices	
Evaluating outcomes	

Handout 1.2A
To the Finish Line

Materials: Handout 1.2B To the Finish Line Game Board for each player; Handout 1.2C To the Finish Line Playing Cards; one prepared deck of cards on cardstock; seven chips for each player

Groups: To be played in groups of two to four students

Purpose: For players to move as many playing pieces as possible to the right of the number lines to reach the finish line

- Each player receives one game board and seven chips.

- Players each place one chip on the zero of each number line on their game board.

- One player shuffles the fraction and decimal cards and places the stack facedown on the table.

- The first player takes the top card and places it faceup on the table. The player may move one or more chips to the right on one or more number lines on the game board as long as the sum of the moves is equal to or less than the value on the card. The player explains the moves, while other players verify that the sum of the moves is equal to or less than the value on the player's card. At the end of each turn, players place the cards in a discard pile.

- The game continues with each player taking a turn.

- If the stack of cards becomes depleted, one player shuffles the cards in the discard pile and places them facedown on the table.

- The winner is the first person to move all of their individual chips to the finish line.

Sample

If the player selected the card ¾, the player may move $.25 + \frac{1}{3} + \frac{1}{6} = \frac{3}{4}$ which is equal to the value on the card. The player might also choose to move $\frac{1}{2} + .1 = .6$, which is less than the value of the card. There are many different combinations that the player may move, as long as the sum of the moves is equal to or less than the value of the card.

Handout 1.2B
To the Finish Line Game Board

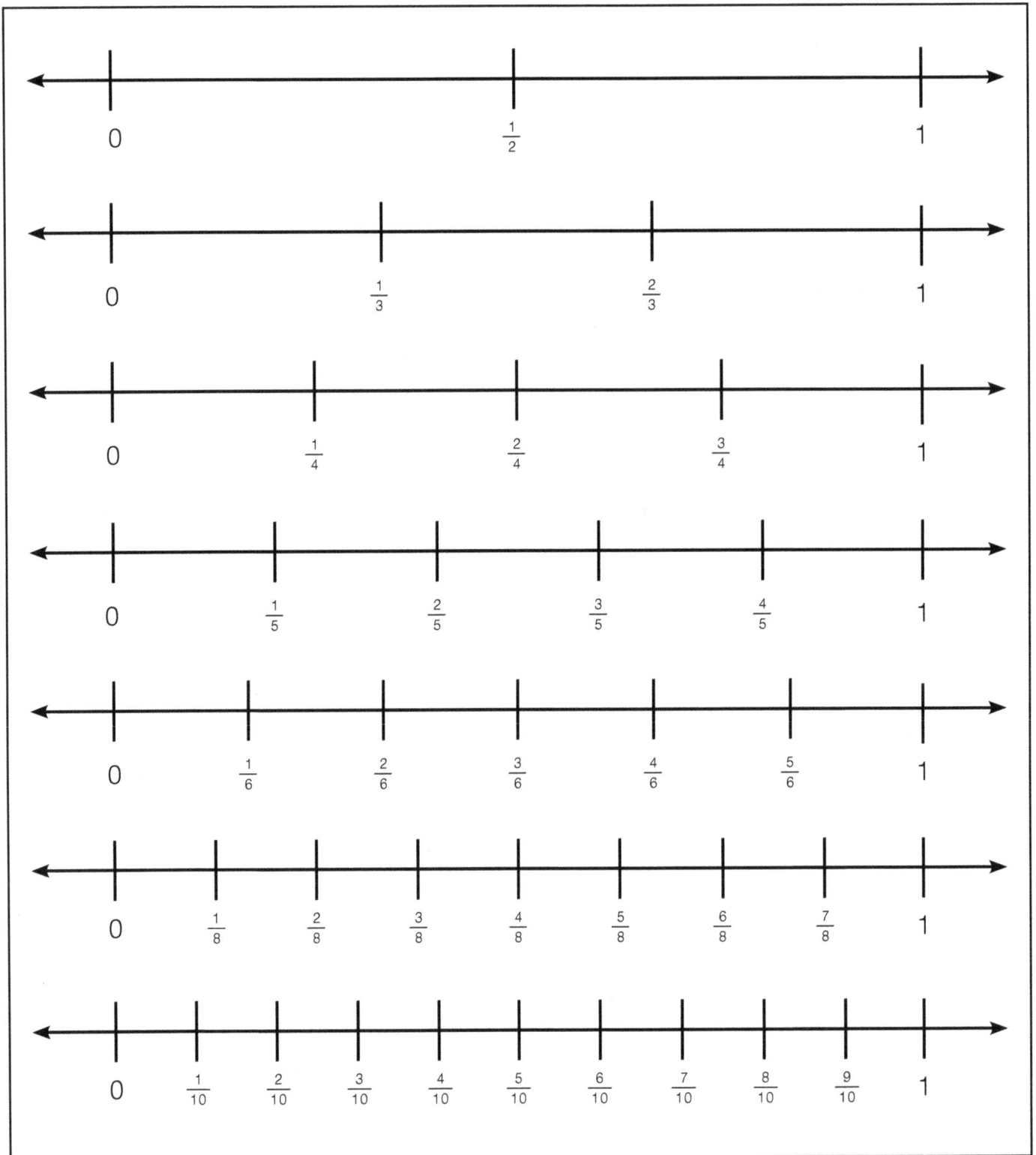

Handout 1.2C

To the Finish Line Playing Cards

$\frac{1}{2}$	$\frac{1}{3}$	$\frac{2}{3}$	$\frac{1}{4}$
$\frac{2}{4}$	$\frac{3}{4}$	$\frac{1}{5}$	$\frac{2}{5}$
$\frac{3}{5}$	$\frac{4}{5}$	$\frac{1}{6}$	$\frac{2}{6}$
$\frac{3}{6}$	$\frac{4}{6}$	$\frac{5}{6}$	$\frac{1}{8}$
$\frac{2}{8}$	$\frac{3}{8}$	$\frac{4}{8}$	$\frac{5}{8}$

$\frac{6}{8}$	$\frac{7}{8}$	$\frac{1}{10}$	$\frac{2}{10}$
$\frac{3}{10}$	$\frac{4}{10}$	$\frac{5}{10}$	$\frac{6}{10}$
$\frac{7}{10}$	$\frac{8}{10}$	$\frac{9}{10}$	2
1	.2	.4	.6
.8	.25	.5	.75

Handout 1.3
Lesson Design Notes

	Ideas and Questions
Where are you now?	
Where do you want to go?	
What is the best way to get there?	

Session 2

Learning Landscape

Overview

How can a learning landscape help teachers understand children's mathematical development?

Description

A learning landscape can function as a "map" of student learning. The landscape may include mathematical big ideas, strategies, and models. Learning does not follow a linear trajectory. Rather, students may move across the learning landscape in different ways as they develop understanding of mathematical concepts.

Key Ideas

- A learning landscape can function as a map of student learning for teachers.
- A learning landscape includes three domains: (1) strategies, (2) big ideas, and (3) mathematical models.

Outline of Activities

- 2.1 What Is a Learning Landscape?   (30 minutes)
- 2.2 Go Fish for Fractions and Decimals   (25 minutes)
- 2.3 Components of a Learning Landscape   (25 minutes)
- 2.4 Before the Next Session   (5 minutes)
- 2.5 Lesson Design Notes   (5 minutes)

What to Bring

- Journal (and writing instruments)

To Complete Before Session 3

- Student Connections: Adding and Subtracting Fractions and Decimals (Handout 2.4)

Facilitator Notes   Session 2

Learning Landscape

If this is your first time facilitating the group, please refer to the more detailed facilitator guidelines in the Introduction. As the facilitator, it is generally your job to keep the conversation flowing and watch the clock. Use your judgment to decide when it's appropriate to extend a session for good conversation or when it's time to move on to the next activity. Remember to keep the group norms posted and revise them, as a group, as necessary.

Before the Session

- Make copies of the following handouts for each team member:
    - ☐ 2.1 Getting From Here to There
    - ☐ 2.2A Go Fish for Fractions and Decimals
    - ☐ 2.2B Go Fish for Fractions and Decimals Playing Cards
    - ☐ 2.3 Components of a Learning Landscape
    - ☐ 2.4 Student Connections: Adding and Subtracting Fractions and Decimals
- Gather the following materials to be used in this session:
    - ☐ Group norms (from Activity 1.4)
    - ☐ Prepared sets of cards (Handout 2.2B) on card stock (see Handout 2.2A)
- Remind team members to bring the following items from previous sessions:
    - ☐ Journal (and writing instruments)

During the Session

- Post group norms, and revise as a group as necessary.
- Activity 2.1: facilitate sharing, and ensure every member has a turn.
- Activity 2.2: facilitate partnering, if necessary; monitor time for games and sharing.
- Activity 2.3: facilitate sharing.

After the Session

- Remind team members of homework, Handout 2.4 Student Connections: Adding and Subtracting Fractions and Decimals.
- Pass any team materials on to the next facilitator.

Activity 2.1 What Is a Learning Landscape?

30 minutes   Handout 2.1 Getting From Here to There

Can you think of a time when you were planning to drive somewhere and needed directions? Before the age of the Internet, most of us relied on maps to plot our routes and to find our way when we got lost. Now it is very common to use electronically generated sets of turn-by-turn directions to get from here to there. On websites like maps.yahoo.com, mapquest.com, and maps.google.com you can print out detailed directions for trips. You can even get real-time turn-by-turn directions by using a portable Global Positioning System (GPS) device in your car. Some might argue that these new navigation tools will eventually make paper maps obsolete.

Think about the kind of information you get when you use turn-by-turn directions compared to the kind of information you get from a printed map. What are the advantages and disadvantages of these two kinds of navigation tools? What do you gain or lose by choosing one navigation mode over the other?

Record your ideas on Handout 2.1.

Discuss how this analogy of navigation relates to teaching.

- In what ways is planning for teaching like planning for a trip?
- What kinds of documents or tools do you use that serve the function of maps or turn-by-turn directions?
- Do you ever feel "lost" when teaching? What do you do about it?
- Do you feel that all of your students are "on the same road" with you?
- Are there particular "landmarks" you watch for in student learning?

Reflect on two of your students, one who is very capable in mathematics and one who struggles with number concepts. **Write** in your journal about the differences between these two students.

- What qualities does the capable student have that the struggling student does not?
- What factors contribute to the success of one student and the challenges of the other?
- Would you say they have similar learning progressions?
- Are they progressing through their mathematical understanding in the same order but at different paces?
- What do you need to know about student learning to help the struggling student catch up with the capable student?
- What do you need to know about student learning in order to continue to challenge the capable student?
- Where is each student on the "travel plan" that you described?

As you may have concluded in your earlier discussion, a scope and sequence document or a textbook that you follow page-by-page could be thought of as a form of turn-by-turn directions for teaching. When you are guided in this way, you don't really have to look ahead; you just turn the page and do what it says. It provides an efficient route to get most students to the goal of learning mathematical concepts and procedures.

However, as with turn-by-turn directions, following a textbook sequence might not provide you with the big picture or map that you need to help *all* students reach the goal of mathematical understanding. As all teachers know, some children take "detours" in their learning or don't start at the point the textbook assumes. If teachers had a map that described how students typically progress in their mathematical understanding, they would have greater flexibility to "adjust the route" because they could plot many paths to get to the final goal. The big picture that lays out what is most important for students to learn and many routes that students might take to get there has thus been called a *landscape of learning.*

Read this quotation describing a landscape of learning.

Landscape of Learning is a metaphor chosen to characterize children's mathematical development. The metaphor of a landscape suggests a picture of a learning terrain in which students move in meandering or direct ways as they develop strategies and ideas about mathematical topics.

Along students' journeys there are moments of uncertainty, moments of potential shifts in understanding (crossroads), and moments where mathematical ideas or strategies are constructed (landmarks).

Knowledge of these moments gives teachers the capacity to better understand, document, and stretch students' thinking.

Maarten Dolk and Catherine Twomey Fosnot,
Fostering Children's Mathematical Development:
The Landscape of Learning (2006, p. vii)

Fosnot and Dolk emphasize that the landscape of learning is not sequential or linear—students follow their own paths as they move around the landscape. As a result, it cannot be used as a checklist of outcomes. This landscape is also fluid, rather than static: "As in any real journey, new landmarks can appear, and new paths, uncharted before, can be carved out. This landscape is simply a representation of others' past journeys—it can inform teaching, but it can also be added to as teachers work with the young mathematicians in their classrooms" (Fosnot & Dolk, 2002, p. 138).

Discuss what this metaphor means to you. How does a landscape of learning relate to the comments you wrote in your journal about the ways planning for teaching is like planning for a trip?

Share what you wrote about your two students with the group. What similarities and differences do you notice in the group's responses? How do the quotes from Dolk and Fosnot and their metaphor of a landscape of learning relate to the variation in student learning that you recorded?

Activity 2.2 Go Fish for Fractions and Decimals

25 minutes

Handout 2.2A Go Fish for Fractions and Decimals

Handout 2.2B Go Fish for Fractions and Decimals Playing Cards

Equivalent fractions and decimals specify the same quantity. Finding equivalent fractions and decimals is an important strategy that students can use to compare, add, and subtract with these types of numbers. To help children develop meaning of equivalent fractions and decimals, they must understand that equivalent fractions represent the same amount even though the representations include different numerators, denominators, and notations.

The object of the Go Fish for Fractions and Decimals game is to collect cards with equivalent values. As you play, consider the strategies you use to determine whether or not two numbers are equivalent.

Read the description of the game on Handout 2.2A.

Play the game in a group of two to four players.

Discuss the following questions:

- What strategies did you use to determine whether or not two numbers are equivalent?
- Which of these strategies are similar to ones that your students use? Which of these strategies are more difficult for students to understand?
- Is this mathematical activity similar to any activities you use in your classroom? Share related activities.
- Is this mathematical activity appropriate for your students? If not, what adaptations could you make to the activity for your students?

Activity 2.3 Components of a Learning Landscape

25 minutes

Handout 2.3 Components of a Learning Landscape

In this activity, you will identify components of a learning landscape for mathematics based on your knowledge of student learning. The learning landscape in mathematics includes three domains: (1) strategies, (2) big ideas, and (3) mathematical models. *Strategies* are the methods that students use to solve problems or to make sense of a situation. *Big ideas* are the important mathematical concepts that form the basis for future learning. *Mathematical models* are physical, visual, and abstract ways to represent mathematical relationships and situations. In the following gray box, you will find some examples of components for each of these domains related to intermediate grades.

Learning Landscape: Domains and Components

Strategies are the methods that students use to solve problems or to make sense of a situation.

Examples

- Using landmark numbers, such as ½, to compare the values of fractions and decimals
- Using multiplication (doubling) or division (halving) to find equivalent fractions
- Using a common whole when comparing, adding, or subtracting with fractions

Big ideas are the important mathematical concepts that form the basis for future learning.

Examples

- Fractions and decimals are used to represent values between whole numbers
- For any given fraction, there are an infinite number of equivalent fractions
- Numbers in the base-ten place value system are related by powers of 10

Mathematical models are physical, visual, and abstract ways to represent mathematical relationships and situations.

Examples

- Base-ten blocks
- Number line
- Ratio table

Handout 2.3 shows a concept web for fractions, decimals, and percents with the three domains of a learning landscape as the branches. This web will serve as a record of the components you identify.

Record some components related to each domain by adding branches to the diagram.

Share your components with each other. Be sure to ask questions so that everyone has a common understanding of the ideas. It may also be helpful to spend some time developing consistent language to describe the components in the three domains.

You will add to this list of components periodically as you move through the sessions in this *Teaching by Design* volume. It is not necessary to completely fill in the concept web at this point. Just be sure to capture the ideas you have so far based on your professional experience at this grade level. This is a document you will return to often, so be sure to staple or tape it in a well-marked place in your journal.

Activity 2.4 Before the Next Session

5 minutes   Handout 2.4 Student Connections: Adding and Subtracting Fractions and Decimals

Before the next session, observe at least three students completing the tasks on Handout 2.4. Ideally you will include the two children you described in Activity 2.1 and at least one additional student. The purpose of this and other Student Connections activities is for you to collect some data about your students that will be shared at the next meeting.

Sit with students individually as they complete the tasks on Handout 2.4 and record what they say and do. Try to be as detailed as possible in describing how they approach the tasks, how difficult the tasks are for the students, what errors they make, and anything else of interest that occurs during the observation.

After you have finished observing three of your students, complete Handout 2.4; make copies of Handout 2.4 and distribute to the remaining students in your class to complete independently. Bring all student work from this activity and your notes to Session 3.

Activity 2.5 Lesson Design Notes

5 minutes

The key ideas for this session are

- A learning landscape can function as a map of student learning for teachers.
- A learning landscape includes three domains: (1) strategies, (2) big ideas, and (3) mathematical models.

Reflect on what you learned during the session and how the ideas apply to each of the three themes in your Lesson Design Notes (Handout 1.3). A few prompts related to the themes follow. These are merely suggestions and should not limit your reflection or the ideas you capture.

- Where do you want to go?
  - In this session, you explored the learning landscape. How might the components of this landscape help you determine where you want to go?
- Where are you now?
  - What might the models or strategies that students use tell you about their current understanding?
- What is the best way to get there?
  - In Activity 2.2, you played Go Fish for Fractions and Decimals. How might you adapt this game to use in your classroom so that each student is supported and challenged in their thinking?

References and Resources

Dolk, M., & Fosnot, C. T. (2006). *Fostering children's mathematical development: The landscape of learning* [CD-ROM]. Portsmouth, NH: Heinemann.

Fosnot, C. T., & Dolk, M. (2002). *Young mathematicians at work: Constructing fractions, decimals, and percents.* Portsmouth, NH: Heinemann.

Handout 2.1
Getting From Here to There

	Maps	Turn-by-Turn Directions
How are they the same?		
Advantages/benefits		
Disadvantages/negatives		

Handout 2.2A
Go Fish for Fractions and Decimals

Materials: Handout 2.2B Go Fish for Fractions and Decimals Playing Cards; one prepared deck of cards on cardstock

Groups: To be played in groups of two to four students

Purpose: For players to collect the most number of cards with equivalent values

- One player shuffles the playing cards and gives five cards to each player.

- Remaining cards are placed facedown in one pile on the table to create a draw pile.

- The player with the last birthday in a calendar year has the first turn.

- Players each examine their hand to see if there are any cards that "match." A match is a pair of cards showing the same value. For example, $\frac{1}{3}$ and $\frac{4}{12}$ form a match. They place all matches in a personal pile, and draw new cards to replace any matches so that each player still has five cards.

- On each player's turn, players select the value of a card in their hand and asks a particular player for a card equivalent in value, "Nora, do you have a card that is equivalent to one half [$\frac{1}{2}$]?"

- If the second player has a card that is equivalent in value, that player gives it to the first player. The first player places the matches in his or her own match pile on the table.

- If no match is made, the second player says, "Go fish." The first player then takes a card from the draw pile.

- It is now the next player's turn.

- If a player runs out of cards, the player draws one card from the draw pile and remains in the game.

- The game continues until all the cards from the draw pile are depleted.

- The player with the most cards in his or her match pile wins the game.

Go Fish for Fractions and Decimals Playing Cards

$\dfrac{1}{2}$	.5	$\dfrac{3}{6}$	$\dfrac{4}{8}$
$\dfrac{1}{3}$	$\dfrac{2}{6}$	$\dfrac{3}{9}$	$\dfrac{4}{12}$
$\dfrac{2}{3}$	$\dfrac{4}{6}$	$\dfrac{10}{15}$	$\dfrac{14}{21}$
$\dfrac{3}{8}$	.25	$\dfrac{3}{12}$	$\dfrac{4}{16}$

$\dfrac{3}{4}$	$\dfrac{6}{8}$	$\dfrac{9}{12}$	.75
$\dfrac{2}{5}$	.4	$\dfrac{4}{10}$	$\dfrac{8}{20}$
$\dfrac{3}{5}$	.6	$\dfrac{6}{10}$	$\dfrac{9}{15}$
$\dfrac{1}{8}$	$\dfrac{2}{16}$	$\dfrac{3}{24}$	.125
$\dfrac{1}{4}$	$\dfrac{6}{16}$	$\dfrac{9}{24}$	.375

Handout 2.3

Components of a Learning Landscape: Fractions and Decimals

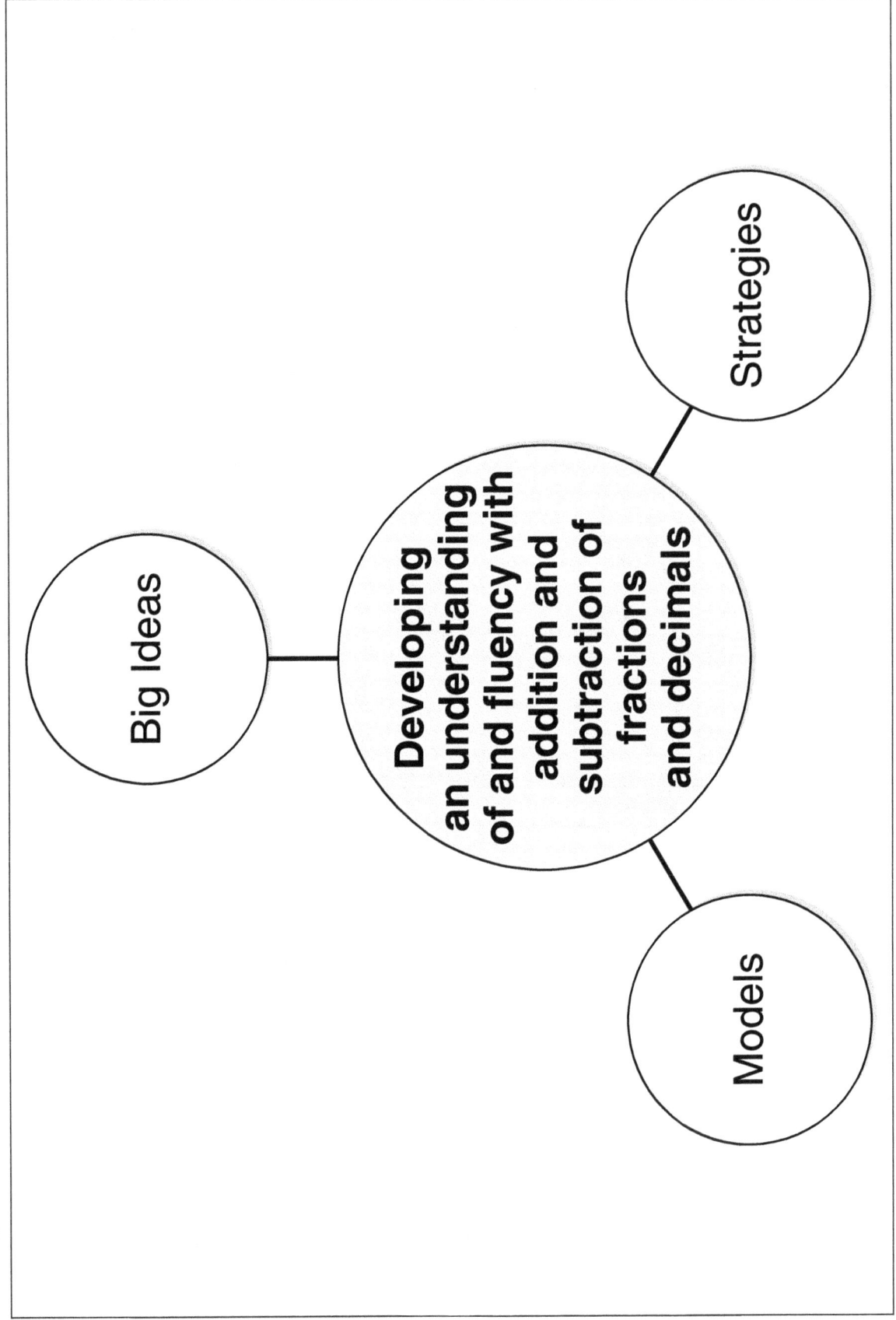

Big Ideas

Developing an understanding of and fluency with addition and subtraction of fractions and decimals

Strategies

Models

Handout 2.4

Student Connections: Adding and Subtracting Fractions and Decimals

Explain how you would find the solutions to each of the problems below. Use pictures (for example: circles, squares, number lines) to help with your explanations.

$\dfrac{1}{2} + \dfrac{1}{3} =$
$\dfrac{2}{3} - \dfrac{1}{6} =$
$1.07 + 4 =$
$2.5 - .38 =$

Session 3

Addition and Subtraction With Like and Related Fractions

Overview

How do children develop skill with adding and subtracting fractions?

Description

Learning to add and subtract fractions is complicated and fraught with computational pitfalls. The procedures for adding and subtracting fractions are difficult to remember when divorced from their conceptual basis. Understanding the learning progression for addition and subtraction with fractions can help teachers to develop effective learning experiences.

Key Ideas

- Developing conceptual understanding about fractions and decimals includes addressing students' misconceptions about rational numbers. Examination of student errors can lead to identification of common sources of misconceptions.

- Student understanding of addition and subtraction with fractions begins with fractions with like denominators, moves to addition and subtraction of fractions with related denominators, and then progresses to proficiency in working with fractions with unlike denominators.

- One-on-one student interviews can provide considerable insight into what children know and can do.

Outline of Activities

- 3.1: The Challenge With Rational Numbers   (30 minutes)
- 3.2: Adding and Subtracting Fractions   (30 minutes)
- 3.3: Conducting Student Interviews   (20 minutes)
- 3.4: Before the Next Session   (5 minutes)
- 3.5: Lesson Design Notes   (5 minutes)

What to Bring

- Journal (and writing instruments)
- Notes and student work: Student Connections activity (Handout 2.4)

To Complete Before Session 4

- Student Connections: Adding and Subtracting Fractions (Handout 3.4)

Facilitator Notes   Session 3

Addition and Subtraction With Like and Related Fractions

If this is your first time facilitating the group, please refer to the more detailed facilitator guidelines in the Introduction. As the facilitator, it is generally your job to keep the conversation flowing and watch the clock. Use your judgment to decide when it's appropriate to extend a session for good conversation or when it's time to move on to the next activity. Remember to keep the group norms posted and revise them, as a group, as necessary.

Before the Session

- Make copies of the following handouts for each team member:
    - ☐ 3.1 Reflecting on Student Learning
    - ☐ 3.2 Adding and Subtracting Fractions With Like, Related, and Unlike Denominators
    - ☐ 3.4 Student Connections: Adding and Subtracting Fractions With Like, Related, and Unlike Denominators
- Gather the following materials to be used in this session:
    - ☐ Group norms (from Activity 1.4)
    - ☐ One or two pairs of scissors
- Remind team members to bring the following items from previous sessions:
    - ☐ Journal (and writing instruments)
    - ☐ Completed homework, Handout 2.4 Student Connections: Adding and Subtracting Fractions and Decimals

During the Session

- Post group norms, and revise as a group as necessary.
- Activity 3.1: facilitate discussion and sharing.
- Activity 3.2: facilitate discussion.
- Activity 3.3: facilitate discussion.

After the Session

- Remind team members of homework, Handout 3.5 Student Connections: Adding and Subtracting Fractions With Like, Related, and Unlike Denominators.
- Pass any team materials on to the next facilitator.

Activity 3.1 The Challenge With Rational Numbers

30 minutes

Handout 2.4 Student Connections: Adding
and Subtracting Fractions and Decimals

Handout 3.1 Reflecting on Student Learning

A rational number is a number that can be expressed exactly as the quotient of two integers (excluding zero as a divisor/denominator). All common fractions and decimals that either terminate (end) or repeat in a pattern (with a set number of digits) are rational numbers. For this reason, we will refer to the set of numbers that includes both fractions and decimals as the set of rational numbers.

For many students, learning about rational numbers is a difficult task. Students who struggle to gain proficiency with rational numbers may develop negative attitudes about mathematics and lose confidence in themselves as mathematicians. In this activity, you will use your knowledge of student learning to identify rational number concepts and procedures that are particularly challenging.

Read the completed Student Connections Handout 2.4 from your class.

Sort your students' papers into piles:

- Place your papers into two piles: pile A for papers with all or mostly correct, and pile B for papers with many errors.

- Further sort pile A by common strategies. Place all the papers where students used a similar approach together in a pile.

- Further sort pile B by errors. Place all the papers with similar errors together in a pile.

Share and compare the results of your work with your group, using the following questions:

- What additional insights did you gain through the sorting process?

- What strategies did students use to solve the problems? Do the strategies indicate a conceptual understanding of fractions and decimals?

- What mathematical misconceptions do children show? Are any of the errors based on inappropriate application of whole number relationships? Are any of the misunderstandings based on incomplete knowledge of place value in the base-ten number system?

- In the Student Connections activity, you observed two students in particular (one high-achiever and one who struggles). Review the notes you took in your journal. What differences did you notice in how the two students approached the problems? Did any students give up or express frustration with the task? Why do you think this was so?

Read the following research quotation:

> Learning about rational numbers is more complicated and difficult than learning about whole numbers. Rational numbers are more complex than whole numbers, in part because they are represented in several ways (e.g., common fractions and decimal fractions) and used in many ways (e.g., as parts of regions and sets, as ratios, as quotients). There are numerous properties for students to learn, including the significant fact that the two numbers that compose a common fraction (numerator and denominator) are related through multiplication and division, not addition. This feature often causes misunderstanding when students first encounter rational numbers. Further, students are likely to have less out-of-school experience with rational numbers than with whole numbers. The result is a number system that presents great challenges to students and teachers. (Kilpatrick, Swafford, & Findell, 2001, p. 231)

Discuss the ideas in the quotation, using the following questions:

- Which of the complexities described pose the greatest challenge to your students? Were any of these in evidence as you sorted through your students' work?

- Are there other challenges related to rational numbers that you would add to this list based on your experience teaching fourth and fifth graders?

Read Handout 3.1 Reflecting on Student Learning.

Discuss and record what your students find easy to learn and understand about fractions and decimals. Then discuss common errors that your students make and the concepts that they find challenging to learn and understand. We will return to fill in the last column in a later session.

- Was your list similar to those of your colleagues?

- What surprised you in the responses from your team members?

- What questions does this raise for you about the development of rational number concepts in fourth and fifth grade students?

Activity 3.2 Adding and Subtracting Fractions

30 minutes

Handout 3.2 Adding and Subtracting Fractions With Like, Related, and Unlike Denominators

Scissors

Read and solve the expressions on Handout 3.2.

Cut apart and sort the problems into three piles according to level of difficulty. That is, which problems would your students find the easiest to solve? Which problems would be the most challenging? Which ones would be "in between" or moderate? Work individually on this task.

Record your sorting and rankings on the problem cards. Write *E* for easy, *M* for moderate, and *C* for challenging.

Compare and discuss your rankings with your group, using the following questions:

- What features did you consider when deciding on your rankings?
- What features do the "easiest" problems have in common?
- What features do the "challenging" problems have in common?
- What features do the "moderate" problems have in common?

Ginsburg, Leinwand, and Decker (2009) outline a set of standards based on the learning progressions they identified for number and operations. Learning progressions describe how students' understanding increases over time as they move from initially naïve to more sophisticated knowledge (National Assessment Governing Board, 2008).

Read the following standards outline for adding and subtracting fractions in Grades 4 and 5 (Ginsburg, Leinwand, & Decker, 2009):

Add and subtract like fractions.	Like fractions have denominators that are the same.	$\frac{3}{4} - \frac{1}{4}$ $\frac{3}{5} + \frac{1}{5}$ $\frac{6}{8} - \frac{3}{8}$ $\frac{3}{7} + \frac{2}{7}$
Add and subtract related fractions.	Related fractions have one denominator that is a factor of the other.	$\frac{1}{3} + \frac{4}{9}$ $\frac{1}{5} + \frac{3}{10}$ $\frac{5}{8} - \frac{1}{4}$ $\frac{1}{2} + \frac{3}{16}$
Add and subtract fractions with unlike denominators.	Fractions with unlike denominators have denominators that are not a factor or multiple of each other.	$\frac{1}{2} - \frac{3}{9}$ $\frac{2}{3} - \frac{1}{5}$ $\frac{2}{5} + \frac{3}{8}$ $\frac{5}{6} - \frac{1}{4}$

Compare your ranked piles with the standards listed above. Did your easy, moderate, and challenging problems fall into these three categories? Which ones were exceptions?

Instructional materials typically treat fractions with like and unlike denominators as two cases for fraction addition; however, breaking the problems into three categories and helping children identify strategies for each of these categories can provide a needed scaffold to mastering fraction addition and subtraction. For problems with related fractions, students often notice that one of the denominators is a factor of the other; therefore, it is easier for students to find a common denominator. For fractions with unlike denominators, equivalent fractions must be found for both fractions in the problem.

Student Connections Activity 3.4 will help you learn more about how your students solve these three types of problems.

Activity 3.3 Conducting Student Interviews

20 minutes

A powerful way to gather formative assessment data about students is through individual interviews. A one-on-one interview provides considerable insight into what children know and can do. Interviews allow the teacher to engage in conversation with each child to determine the extent of knowledge and the relative sophistication of the child's numerical strategies. By asking probing questions, teachers can encourage students to clarify their interpretations of the problem and their responses. During the interviews, a teacher gathers data about the problem-solving strategies and thinking processes that students use to approach each problem. By interviewing many students, teachers gather information about the misconceptions their students have and the range of strategies that they use to solve mathematics problems.

Interviews provide teachers with a detailed picture of children's mathematical understanding and therefore help them to improve their practice (Buschman, 2001). However, conducting one-on-one interviews also presents some challenges. It takes specialized skill and practice to become proficient in using interviews to guide instruction.

Reflect on the three student interviews you conducted. What new insights do you have about these children? What new questions do you have about their understanding of fractions and decimals? What went well with the interviews? What challenges did you face?

Brainstorm a list of suggestions for conducting student interviews based on your shared responses to the questions above. What advice do you have for yourself or for a colleague who might embark on mathematical interviews with students?

Read the following suggestions for conducting student interviews that come from mathematics education experts.

Prepare for the interviews.

Choose a private location where distractions can be minimized. Try to ensure that you and the children will not be interrupted during the interviews. Provide a range of tools, including various manipulatives, pencils, paper, and so on.

Select tasks and problems with care.

Pose a problem that will challenge students. Prepare several tasks that range in difficulty. If the student quickly solves the problem, provide a more challenging problem. If the student cannot complete the given tasks, try one that is slightly easier. However, be sure to provide enough time for students to struggle and make sense of the problem. You may also suggest that they try using a different tool before moving to an easier task.

Listen carefully.

The child should do most of the talking, not you. Of course, you have to ask penetrating questions, but you should spend most of your time listening to what the child has to say and observing. If you are talking more than the child, something is wrong. Try to search for the child's point of view. Extending or expanding a child's thinking is difficult until you first determine how a child approaches the problem. Most children also think differently than adults do, which means that seeing the problem from a child's point of view can be challenging.

Ask the right questions.

Phrase your questions in a neutral way so as to avoid suggesting an answer to a child. Pay attention to non-verbal cues as well—tone and facial expressions can be quite revealing. Start with open-ended questions, and then proceed to more specific questions as you gain insight into the reasons behind children's thinking. Some questions you may consider include, "How did you think about this problem?" or, "What did you do to get this answer?"

Don't correct and teach.

When a student makes a mistake or has an incorrect solution, your goal is to determine the child's mathematical thinking, not to correct thinking. Later on you will have an opportunity to use what you learned in the interview to help the child. Refrain from correcting and teaching. Avoid saying, "No, you're wrong; this is how to do it." Don't show your disapproval by grimacing or scowling. Instead, convey your interest in what the child said, even if it is wrong, and that you want to find out more about it.

Sources: Ginsburg, Jacobs, & Lopez, 1998; Buschman, 2001.

Discuss the following questions:

- How does your list compare to this list?
- Which suggestions are the most helpful for you?
- When you consider both your list and the items from the mathematics education experts, what are some of the challenges you might face in attempting to abide by these guidelines?

Activity 3.4 Before the Next Session

5 minutes

Handout 3.2 Adding and Subtracting Fractions With Like,
Related, and Unlike Denominators
Handout 3.4 Student Connections: Adding and
Subtracting Fractions With Like, Related, and Unlike Denominators

Student Interviews

Before the next session, pose some of the problems you sorted in this session on Handout 3.2 to several of your students. Pose at least one "easy" problem, one "moderate" problem, and one "challenging" problem. You should feel free to alter the values in the problems to appropriately meet students' needs, using like and related denominators for struggling students, and using related and unlike denominators to find the limits of higher-achieving students. Again, the purpose of conducting the interviews is to find the mathematical limit for each of your students. Use Handout 3.4 to record the problems you choose and the difficulty rankings. There is also space to record your notes about how students solve the problems. Using your students' responses, be prepared to report in the next session whether you would like to change the difficulty ranking you originally made for any of the problems.

Activity 3.5 Lesson Design Notes

5 minutes

The key ideas for this session are

- Developing conceptual understanding about fractions and decimals includes addressing students' misconceptions about rational numbers. Examination of student errors can lead to identification of common sources of misconceptions.

- Student understanding of addition and subtraction with fractions begins with fractions with like denominators, moves to addition and subtraction of fractions with related denominators, and then progresses to proficiency in working with fractions with unlike denominators.

- One-on-one student interviews can provide considerable insight into what children know and can do.

Reflect on what you learned during this session and how the ideas apply to each of the three themes in your Lesson Design Notes (Handout 1.3). A few prompts related to the themes follow. These are merely suggestions and should not limit your reflection or the ideas you capture.

- Where do you want to go?
  - In Activity 3.2, you discussed a learning progression for adding and subtracting fractions. How might this learning progression inform where you want your students to go?

- Where are you now?
  o In Activity 3.1, you discussed student connections. What new insights do you have about your students' understanding of fractions and decimals?
- What is the best way to get there?
  o In Activity 3.2, you explored "easy," "moderate," and "challenging" addition and subtraction problems. How might you use these different types of problems in your lessons on adding and subtracting fractions?

References and Resources

Buschman, L. (2001). Using student interviews to guide classroom instruction: An action research project. *Teaching Children Mathematics, 8*(4), 222–227.

Ginsburg, A., Leinwand, S., & Decker, K. (2009). *Informing Grades 1–6 standards development: What can be learned from high-performing Hong Kong, Korea, and Singapore?* Washington, DC: American Institutes for Research.

Ginsburg, H. P., Jacobs, S., & Lopez, L. (1998). *The teacher's guide to flexible interviewing in the classroom: Learning what children know about math.* Needham Heights, MA: Allyn & Bacon.

Kilpatrick, J., Swafford, J., & Findell, B. (Eds.). (2001). *Adding it up: Helping children learn mathematics.* Washington, DC: National Academies Press.

National Assessment Governing Board. (2008). *National Assessment of Educational Progress (NAEP) 2009 science framework.* (ED–04–CO–0148). Washington, DC: Author.

Handout 3.1

Reflecting on Student Learning

Work with others in your group to discuss and record what your students find easy to learn and understand about fractions and decimals. Then, discuss common errors that your students make and the concepts that they find challenging to learn and understand.

Concepts	My students typically find it easy to . . .	My students often make these errors and have the following misconceptions:	
Understanding the value of fractions and decimals			
Comparing the values among and between fractions and decimals			
Finding equivalent fractions or decimals			
Adding and subtracting with fractions or decimals			

Adding and Subtracting Fractions With Like, Related, and Unlike Denominators

$\dfrac{1}{2} + \dfrac{3}{9}$	$\dfrac{1}{2} - \dfrac{3}{16}$	$\dfrac{1}{3} + \dfrac{4}{9}$
$\dfrac{2}{5} + \dfrac{3}{8}$	$\dfrac{3}{4} - \dfrac{1}{4}$	$\dfrac{5}{6} - \dfrac{1}{4}$
$\dfrac{1}{5} + \dfrac{3}{10}$	$\dfrac{3}{7} + \dfrac{2}{7}$	$\dfrac{2}{3} - \dfrac{1}{5}$
$\dfrac{3}{5} + \dfrac{1}{5}$	$\dfrac{5}{8} - \dfrac{1}{4}$	$\dfrac{6}{8} - \dfrac{3}{8}$

Handout 3.4

Student Connections: Adding and Subtracting Fractions With Like, Related, and Unlike Denominators

Select several problems from Handout 3.2 to pose to each of three students. Select a variety of "easy," "moderate," and "challenging" problems to collect information on the mathematical limit for each student. Provide blank paper and pencils, and allow students to use any method to solve these problems. Take notes here about the strategies they use to solve the problems.

Student 1	
Problem A:	
Level of difficulty:	
Problem B:	
Level of difficulty:	
Problem C:	
Level of difficulty:	

Student 2	
Problem A:	
Level of difficulty:	
Problem B:	
Level of difficulty:	
Problem C:	
Level of difficulty:	
Student 3	
Problem A:	
Level of difficulty:	
Problem B:	
Level of difficulty:	
Problem C:	
Level of difficulty:	

Session 4

Understanding Equivalent Fractions

Overview

How can students develop conceptual understanding of equivalent fractions?

Description

Understanding equivalent fractions is an important concept that leads to strong conceptual understanding of addition and subtraction of fractions. The notion that the same fractional value can be named in an infinite number of ways forms the conceptual and procedural foundation for addition and subtraction of fractions. Teachers can use manipulatives and puzzles to strengthen students' understanding of equivalent fractions.

Key Ideas

- Students' understanding of fractional equivalence is strengthened when they have many opportunities to explore the concept that a given fractional value can be named in many ways.

- Students with a deep understanding of rational numbers will develop flexible and efficient strategies for finding fraction equivalents that include numerical reasoning.

- The Standards for Mathematical Practice in the Common Core State Standards identify areas of instructional emphasis and help to make connections between different mathematical concepts and processes.

- When instruction focuses on a small number of key areas of emphasis, students gain extended experience with core concepts and skills.

Outline of Activities

- 4.1 Analyzing Student Connections (15 minutes)
- 4.2 Finding Equivalent Fractions Using the Same Whole (25 minutes)
- 4.3 Finding Equivalent Fractions When the Whole Is Unknown (25 minutes)

- 4.4 The Common Core State Standards   (15 minutes)
- 4.5 Before the Next Session   (5 minutes)
- 4.6 Lesson Design Notes   (5 minutes)

What to Bring

- Journal (and writing instruments)
- Notes and student work: Student Connections activity (Handout 3.4)

To Complete Before Session 5

- Investigating Instructional Materials activity with NCTM Illuminations

Facilitator Notes   Session 4

Understanding Equivalent Fractions

If this is your first time facilitating the group, please refer to the more detailed facilitator guidelines in the Introduction. As the facilitator, it is generally your job to keep the conversation flowing and watch the clock. Use your judgment to decide when it's appropriate to extend a session for good conversation or when it's time to move on to the next activity. Remember to keep the group norms posted and revise them, as a group, as necessary.

Before the Session

- Make copies of the following handout for each team member:
    - ☐ 4.4 Common Core State Standards
- Gather the following materials to be used in this session:
    - ☐ Group norms (from Activity 1.4)
    - ☐ Square color tiles in yellow, green, and blue
- Remind team members to bring the following items:
    - ☐ Journal (and writing instruments)
    - ☐ Handouts 3.1 and 3.2
    - ☐ Completed homework, Handout 3.4 Student Connections: Adding and Subtracting Fractions With Like, Related, and Unlike Denominators

During the Session

- Post group norms, and revise as a group as necessary.
- Activity 4.1: facilitate sharing.
- Activity 4.2: facilitate discussion and sharing.
- Activity 4.3: facilitate partnering, if necessary.

After the Session

- Remind team members of homework, to teach a lesson or activity from NCTM's Illuminations website.
- Pass any team materials to the next facilitator.

Activity 4.1 Analyzing Student Connections

15 minutes

Handout 3.2 Adding and Subtracting Fractions
Handout 3.4 Student Connections: Adding and
Subtracting Fractions With Like, Related, and Unlike Denominators

One of your tasks from the previous session was to pose the problems from Handout 3.2 to your students. You were to pose at least one "easy" problem, one "moderate" problem, and one "challenging" problem.

Share the results with your group, using the following questions:

- Which problem(s) did you identify as easy? Did your students find them easy to solve?

- Which problem(s) did you identify as moderate? Did your students struggle more with these problems?

- Which problem(s) did you identify as challenging? Were your students able to solve them?

- Based on your shared results, should you change any of your difficulty rankings? If so, change the letter (*E, M,* or *C*) on the handout.

- Where did your students fall on the learning progression for addition and subtraction with fractions: like fractions, related fractions, or unlike fractions?

You will be analyzing and discussing student strategies for addition and subtraction in future sessions. Save Handouts 3.2 and 3.4 for these discussions.

Activity 4.2 Finding Equivalent Fractions Using the Same Whole

25 minutes

Understanding how and why we can name a given fractional portion with an infinite number of equivalent fraction names is an important concept that students need to internalize in order to develop strategies and procedures for adding, and subtracting, fractions (Wong & Evans, 2007). The central idea students must understand is that different fractions can name the same quantity even though they include different numerators and denominators.

Read the following classroom vignette that includes modeling and describes how three students identify a fraction to represent the gray tiles in a set of 24.

Classroom Vignette

Ms. Everett: You each have a collection of tiles on your desk. Some of these tiles are white and some of them are gray. What fractions can you find to represent the portion of tiles that are gray?

Charlie: I counted all of the tiles and there are 24 tiles altogether, and 4 of them are gray. So, four–twenty-fourths [$\frac{4}{24}$] of the tiles are gray.

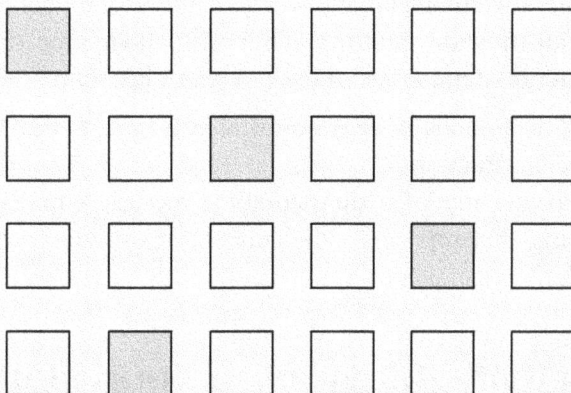

David: I put the tiles into groups of 2 and made 12 groups, and 2 of the groups are gray. Two-twelfths [$\frac{2}{12}$] of the tiles are gray.

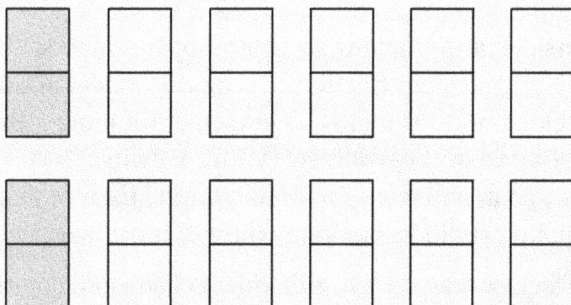

Sarah: I put the tiles into groups of 4 and there are 6 groups. One of these groups of 4 is gray. So one-sixth [$\frac{1}{6}$] of the tiles are gray.

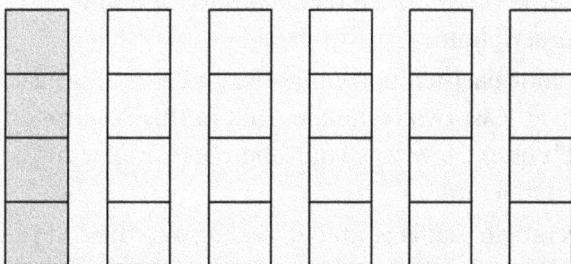

Discuss the following questions:

- How are David's and Sarah's strategies different from Charlie's strategy?
- The three students described the portion of gray tiles using the fractions $\frac{4}{24}$, $\frac{2}{12}$, and $\frac{1}{6}$. How might you facilitate discussion among these students to get them to explain to each other that these are equivalent fractions? What might be confusing and serve as a challenge in understanding that these are equivalent fractions?
- If you were Ms. Everett, how would you extend this lesson to help children solidify their understanding of equivalent fractions?
- How might you "reverse" the process above to help students find additional equivalent fractions?
- In this example, arrangements of square tiles serve as a model representing equivalent fractional names for the same quantity. What other models for fraction equivalence have you seen in instructional materials or used in your classroom?

Share a brief summary of an activity or lesson that you have found effective in helping students understand equivalent fractions.

The vignette incorporates use of a mathematical model. A mathematical model is any object, picture, or drawing that represents the concept or on which the relationship for that concept can be imposed.

Activity 4.3 Finding Equivalent Fractions When the Whole Is Unknown

25 minutes

Handout 3.1 Reflecting on Student Learning
Square colored tiles in yellow, green, and blue

In Activity 4.2, you considered multiple ways to group the same set of tiles into equal-sized parts as a way to represent equivalent fractions. Using this model in this way lays the foundation for a more sophisticated understanding of equivalent fractions that requires students to determine the number of items in the whole set (Wong & Evans, 2007).

In this activity, your group will work on a few puzzles, then read and discuss some classroom conversations depicting students working on the same puzzle.

Try these tasks yourself before reading the subsequent classroom conversations. As you work, be aware of your thought processes in solving the puzzles.

- Using colored tiles, first build a rectangle that is $\frac{1}{2}$ green, $\frac{1}{4}$ blue, and the rest yellow. Once you have built one rectangle that fits this description, share your results with a partner. Did you build the same rectangle? If not, how do they differ? Now see if the two of you can build at least two more rectangles (with a different number of tiles in each one) that fit this description.
- Continuing with your partner, now build rectangles that are $\frac{1}{2}$ green, $\frac{1}{3}$ blue, and the rest yellow. Create at least two rectangles that fit this description (with a different number of tiles in each one). How was your approach similar to your approach to the first puzzle? How was it different?
- Finally, build a rectangle that is $\frac{2}{5}$ green, $\frac{1}{3}$ blue, and the rest yellow. Once you have created one rectangle that fits this description, describe a rule or process that would allow you to create another and another (each using a different number of tiles).

Classroom Conversations

The tasks you have just completed were also completed by students in Ms. Herrera's class.

Ms. Herrera: Using your tiles, build a rectangle that is two-fifths [$\frac{2}{5}$] green, one-third [$\frac{1}{3}$] blue, and the rest yellow.

During work time, Ms. Herrera overheard this conversation between Daniel and Serena:

Serena: The first fraction is fifths and we have 2 of them. That means we need 2 groups of 5.

Daniel: Okay, and the second fraction is thirds but we only have 1 of them. Add 3 more tiles.

Serena: Now we have 13 tiles all together. So . . .

Daniel: Add 2 yellow tiles. Now we have 15 total, and 2 are yellow.

Serena: With 15 tiles, two-fifteenths [$\frac{2}{15}$] is the yellow portion.

Here is another conversation Ms. Herrera overheard between Aidan and Thomas:

Aidan: Let's start with 5 tiles so we can break it into fifths. But we can't break 5 tiles into 3 parts to show thirds.

Thomas: Unless we cut the tiles, but I don't think we're allowed to do that. Let's try 10 tiles because we can split 10 tiles into fifths.

Aidan: Yeah, but we still can't break that into thirds.

Thomas: Wait, I see it now. We can use 15 tiles . . . 3 groups of 5, 5 groups of 3 . . . yes, that works with both fifths and thirds! That's right, 3 times 5 is 15.

Ms. Herrera also overheard this conversation between Petra and Mike:

Mike: This is an impossible problem. You can't build something that shows fifths and thirds.

Petra: Yeah, I mean how can you cut 5 tiles into 3 parts or 3 tiles into 5 parts? It just won't work . . . unless we can cut the tiles into pieces. I think this is a trick question.

Ms. Herrera also overheard this conversation between Tyler and Savannah:

Tyler: Let's try using 30 tiles because 30 can be divided into 3 equal groups of 10 and 5 equal groups of 6.

Savannah: Okay, since one-third [$\frac{1}{3}$] of 30 is 10, make 10 of the tiles blue.

Tyler: Yeah, and one-fifth [$\frac{1}{5}$] of 30 is 6 which means two-fifths [$\frac{2}{5}$] of 30 is 12.

Savannah: And 10 plus 12 is 22, so we still need 8 more tiles to make 30. I guess that means there are 8 yellow tiles.

Tyler: Eight-thirtieths [$\frac{8}{30}$] is yellow.

Savannah: I think we must have done something wrong because I heard another group say they got four-fifteenths [$\frac{4}{15}$] yellow. Maybe we should try again.

Describe the strategies Ms. Herrera observed with these students, using the following questions:

- Which of the strategies will lead to a correct solution?

- How would you respond to Daniel and Serena? What questions could you ask them to further their thinking without giving them a solution?

- How would you respond to Mike and Petra? What questions could you ask them to further their thinking without giving them a solution?

- How would you respond to Tyler and Savannah? How does the model from Activity 4.2 relate to their confusion?

- How might joining pairs of students for additional discussion help them clarify equivalent fraction concepts? Which pairs of students would you combine?

Revisit Handout 3.1. Label the final column "Strategies." Read each of the cells in the first column. Add any strategies that have been discussed that would be helpful for each of the categories. Continue to add strategies as they are discussed in future sessions.

Activity 4.4 The Common Core State Standards

15 minutes   Handout 4.4 Common Core State Standards

Discuss the following questions with your group:

- Have you heard or used the phrase *a mile wide and an inch deep* when talking about curriculum? What does this phrase mean to you?

- How well does this phrase describe your own experience as a mathematical learner?

- What are the problems associated with curriculum that covers lots of topics, but none in depth?

Read the following excerpt from the Introduction to the Common Core State Standards for Mathematics.

For over a decade, research studies of mathematics education in high-performing countries have pointed to the conclusion that the mathematics curriculum in the United States must become substantially more focused and coherent in order to improve mathematics achievement in this country. To deliver on the promise of common standards, the standards must address the problem of a curriculum that is "a mile wide and an inch deep." These Standards are a substantial answer to that challenge.

It is important to recognize that "fewer standards" are no substitute for focused standards. Achieving "fewer standards" would be easy to do by resorting to broad, general statements. Instead, these Standards aim for clarity and specificity.

Assessing the coherence of a set of standards is more difficult than assessing their focus. William Schmidt and Richard Houang (2002) have said that content standards and curricula are coherent if they are:

articulated over time as a sequence of topics and performances that are logical and reflect, where appropriate, the sequential or hierarchical nature of the disciplinary content from which the subject matter derives. That is, what and how students are taught should reflect not only the topics that fall within a certain academic discipline, **but also the key ideas** [emphasis added] that determine how knowledge is organized and generated within that discipline. This implies that "to be coherent," a set of content standards must evolve from particulars (e.g., the meaning and operations of whole numbers, including simple math facts and routine computational procedures associated with whole numbers and fractions) to deeper structures inherent in the discipline. These deeper structures then serve as a means for connecting the particulars (such as an understanding of the rational number system and its properties).

These Standards endeavor to follow such a design, not only by stressing conceptual understanding of key ideas, but also by continually returning to organizing principles such as place value or the laws of arithmetic to structure those ideas.

In addition, the "sequence of topics and performances" that is outlined in a body of mathematics standards must also respect what is known about how students learn. As Confrey (2007) points out, developing "sequenced obstacles and challenges for students . . . absent the insights about meaning that derive from careful study of learning, would be unfortunate and unwise." In recognition of this, the development of these Standards began with research-based learning progressions detailing what is known today about how students' mathematical knowledge, skill, and understanding develop over time.

Source: National Governors Association Center for Best Practices and Council of Chief State School Officers (2010, p. 3)

Discuss the following questions with your group:

- How do the Common Core State Standards attempt to address the problem of a curriculum that is "a mile wide and an inch deep"?
- What does it mean to have content standards that are coherent?

The Common Core State Standards for Mathematics begin with eight Standards for Mathematical Practice. These standards describe processes and proficiencies with longstanding importance in mathematics and apply across all of the grades from kindergarten to Grade 12.

Read the Standards for Mathematical Practice (Handout 4.4).

Write in your journal, in response to the following questions:

- Which of the eight Standards for Mathematical Practice have you intentionally designed instruction to support?
- Which of the eight Standards for Mathematical Practice are challenging to teach and not typically present in your classroom?
- What ideas do you have for increasing students' opportunities to develop and use the practices described by these standards?

Share with your group your responses to the third question in the preceding list.

If you do not have a copy of the Standards for Mathematical Content for your grade, go to the website at http://www.corestandards.org/ and print a copy. You will use it as a resource in subsequent sessions. If you would like to learn more about the Common Core State Standards, review other documentation provided on the website. For example, the "Myths and Facts" document and the FAQ section provide helpful information.

Activity 4.5 Before the Next Session

5 minutes

Before Session 5, visit NCTM's Illuminations website (http://illuminations.nctm.org/) and identify an activity or lesson to try in your classroom. According to NCTM, the site is designed to accomplish the following:

- Provide standards-based resources that improve the teaching and learning of mathematics for all students.
- Provide materials that illuminate the vision for school mathematics set forth in *Principles and Standards for School Mathematics.*

The Illuminations site includes four sections: activities, lessons, standards, and web links. For this activity, use the activities or lessons sections for your search. Try to find a lesson that is related to fractions or decimals for the fourth or fifth grade. You may want to work in pairs to plan and implement the activity or lesson.

Before you use the lesson, write in your journal about your goals and expectations. Consider the following questions:

- Why did you choose this lesson or activity?
- What is the goal or learning objective for the lesson or activity?
- How is the lesson or activity connected to the components of a learning landscape or the Common Core State Standards?
- How do you think students will respond to the tasks?
- What modifications will you make?

After you teach the lesson or use the activity, collect student work or other artifacts. Take some time to reflect on what happened. Write responses to the following questions in your journal:

- What aspects of the activity or lesson were successful?
- What aspects of the lessons went according to your expectations? Were there any unexpected reactions from students?
- What evidence do you have that students met the goal?

- What was challenging about using the lesson?
- What would you do differently? How would you advise other teachers who want to use the lesson?

You will share the results in Session 5. You will also use the results of this activity to design the prototype lesson. Save your materials, student work, and reflections for Session 12 as well.

Activity 4.6 Lesson Design Notes

5 minutes

The key ideas for this session are

- Students' understanding of fractional equivalence is strengthened when they have many opportunities to explore the concept that a given fractional value can be named in many ways.
- Students with a deep understanding of rational numbers will develop flexible and efficient strategies for finding fraction equivalents that include numerical reasoning.
- The Standards for Mathematical Practice in the Common Core State Standards identify areas of instructional emphasis and help to make connections between different mathematical concepts and processes.
- When instruction focuses on a small number of key areas of emphasis, students gain extended experience with core concepts and skills.

Reflect on what you learned during this session and how the ideas apply to each of the three themes in your Lesson Design Notes. A few prompts related to the themes follow. These are merely suggestions and should not limit your reflection or the ideas you capture.

- Where do you want to go?
  o In Activity 4.4, you discussed the Common Core State Standards. What connections do you see between the standards and your notes related to this question? What ideas from the standards can be included in your notes?

- Where are you now?
  o In Activity 4.1, you shared and discussed the results of your student connections. Which fraction problems are your students able to solve easily? Which problems are challenging?
  o In Activities 4.2 and 4.3, you read and discussed vignettes describing strategies students used to find equivalent fractions. Are there any insights from this process that will inform how you identify your students' current knowledge about a mathematical concept?

- What is the best way to get there?
  o In Activities 4.2 and 4.3, you explored the use of colored tiles as a model for fractions. How can this model be used to support students in developing understanding of equivalent fractions?

References and Resources

Fosnot, C. T., & Dolk, M. (2002). *Young mathematicians at work: Constructing fractions, decimals and percents.* Portsmouth, NH: Heinemann.

Lamon, S. J. (1999). *Teaching fractions and ratios for understanding.* Mahwah, NJ: Lawrence Erlbaum.

National Governors Association Center for Best Practices, & Council of Chief State School Officers. (2010). *Common Core State Standards: Mathematics.* Retrieved from http://www.corestandards.org/the-standards/mathematics/

Wong, M., & Evans, D. (2007). Students' conceptual understanding of equivalent fractions. In J. Watson & K. Beswick (Eds.), *Mathematics: Essential research, essential practice. Proceedings of the 30th annual conference of the Mathematics Education Research Group of Australasia* (Vol. 1, pp. 824–833). Adelaide, Australia: MERGA.

Handout 4.4
Common Core State Standards

Mathematics | Standards for Mathematical Practice

The Standards for Mathematical Practice describe varieties of expertise that mathematics educators at all levels should seek to develop in their students. These practices rest on important "processes and proficiencies" with longstanding importance in mathematics education. The first of these are the NCTM process standards of problem solving, reasoning and proof, communication, representation, and connections. The second are the strands of mathematical proficiency specified in the National Research Council's report *Adding It Up:* adaptive reasoning, strategic competence, conceptual understanding (comprehension of mathematical concepts, operations and relations), procedural fluency (skill in carrying out procedures flexibly, accurately, efficiently and appropriately), and productive disposition (habitual inclination to see mathematics as sensible, useful, and worthwhile, coupled with a belief in diligence and one's own efficacy).

1. Make sense of problems and persevere in solving them.

Mathematically proficient students start by explaining to themselves the meaning of a problem and looking for entry points to its solution. They analyze givens, constraints, relationships, and goals. They make conjectures about the form and meaning of the solution and plan a solution pathway rather than simply jumping into a solution attempt. They consider analogous problems, and try special cases and simpler forms of the original problem in order to gain insight into its solution. They monitor and evaluate their progress and change course if necessary. Older students might, depending on the context of the problem, transform algebraic expressions or change the viewing window on their graphing calculator to get the information they need. Mathematically proficient students can explain correspondences between equations, verbal descriptions, tables, and graphs or draw diagrams of important features and relationships, graph data, and search for regularity or trends. Younger students might rely on using concrete objects or pictures to help conceptualize and solve a problem. Mathematically proficient students check their answers to problems using a different method, and they continually ask themselves, "Does this make sense?" They can understand the approaches of others to solving complex problems and identify correspondences between different approaches.

2. Reason abstractly and quantitatively.

Mathematically proficient students make sense of quantities and their relationships in problem situations. They bring two complementary abilities to bear on problems involving quantitative relationships: the ability to *decontextualize*—to abstract a given situation and represent it symbolically and manipulate the representing symbols as if they have a life of their own, without necessarily attending to their referents—and the ability to *contextualize,* to pause as needed during the manipulation process in order to probe into the referents for the symbols involved. Quantitative reasoning entails habits of creating a coherent representation of the problem at hand; considering the units involved; attending to the meaning of quantities, not just how to compute them; and knowing and flexibly using different properties of operations and objects.

3. Construct viable arguments and critique the reasoning of others.

Mathematically proficient students understand and use stated assumptions, definitions, and previously established results in constructing arguments. They make conjectures and build a logical progression of statements to explore the truth of their conjectures. They are able to analyze situations by breaking them into cases, and can recognize and use counterexamples. They justify their conclusions, communicate them to others, and respond to the arguments of others. They reason inductively about data, making plausible arguments that take into account the context from which the data arose. Mathematically proficient students are also able to compare the effectiveness of two plausible arguments, distinguish correct logic or reasoning from that which is flawed, and—if there is a flaw in an argument—explain what it is. Elementary students can construct arguments using concrete referents such as objects, drawings, diagrams, and actions. Such arguments can make sense and be correct, even though they are not generalized or made formal until later grades. Later, students learn to determine domains to which an argument applies. Students at all grades can listen or read the arguments of others, decide whether they make sense, and ask useful questions to clarify or improve the arguments.

4. Model with mathematics.

Mathematically proficient students can apply the mathematics they know to solve problems arising in everyday life, society, and the workplace. In early grades, this might be as simple as writing an addition equation to describe a situation. In middle grades, a student might apply proportional reasoning to plan a school event or analyze a problem in the community. By high school, a student might use geometry to solve a design problem or use a function to describe how one quantity of interest depends on another. Mathematically proficient students who can apply what they know are comfortable making assumptions and approximations to simplify a complicated situation, realizing that these may need revision later. They are able to identify important quantities in a practical situation and map their relationships using such tools as diagrams, two-way tables, graphs, flowcharts and formulas. They can analyze those relationships mathematically to draw conclusions. They routinely interpret their mathematical results in the context of the situation and reflect on whether the results make sense, possibly improving the model if it has not served its purpose.

5. Use appropriate tools strategically.

Mathematically proficient students consider the available tools when solving a mathematical problem. These tools might include pencil and paper, concrete models, a ruler, a protractor, a calculator, a spreadsheet, a computer algebra system, a statistical package, or dynamic geometry software. Proficient students are sufficiently familiar with tools appropriate for their grade or course to make sound decisions about when each of these tools might be helpful, recognizing both the insight to be gained and their limitations. For example, mathematically proficient high school students analyze graphs of functions and solutions generated using a graphing calculator. They detect possible errors by strategically using estimation and other mathematical knowledge. When making mathematical models, they know that technology can enable them to visualize the results of varying assumptions, explore consequences, and compare predictions with data. Mathematically proficient students at various grade levels are able to identify relevant external mathematical resources, such as digital content located on a website, and use them to pose or solve problems. They are able to use technological tools to explore and deepen their understanding of concepts.

6. Attend to precision.

Mathematically proficient students try to communicate precisely to others. They try to use clear definitions in discussion with others and in their own reasoning. They state the meaning of the symbols they choose, including using the equal sign consistently and appropriately. They are careful about specifying units of measure, and labeling axes to clarify the correspondence with quantities in a problem. They calculate accurately and efficiently, express numerical answers with a degree of precision appropriate for the problem context. In the elementary grades, students give carefully formulated explanations to each other. By the time they reach high school they have learned to examine claims and make explicit use of definitions.

7. Look for and make use of structure.

Mathematically proficient students look closely to discern a pattern or structure. Young students, for example, might notice that three and seven more is the same amount as seven and three more, or they may sort a collection of shapes according to how many sides the shapes have. Later, students will see 7×8 equals the well remembered $7 \times 5 + 7 \times 3$, in preparation for learning about the distributive property. In the expression $x^2 + 9x + 14$, older students can see the 14 as 2×7 and the 9 as $2 + 7$. They recognize the significance of an existing line in a geometric figure and can use the strategy of drawing an auxiliary line for solving problems. They also can step back for an overview and shift perspective. They can see complicated things, such as some algebraic expressions, as single objects or as being composed of several objects. For example, they can see $5 - 3(x - y)^2$ as 5 minus a positive number times a square and use that to realize that its value cannot be more than 5 for any real numbers x and y.

8. Look for and express regularity in repeated reasoning.

Mathematically proficient students notice if calculations are repeated, and look both for general methods and for shortcuts. Upper elementary students might notice when dividing 25 by 11 that they are repeating the same calculations over and over again, and conclude they have a repeating decimal. By paying attention to the calculation of slope as they repeatedly check whether points are on the line through (1, 2) with slope 3, middle school students might abstract the equation $(y - 2)/(x - 1) = 3$. Noticing the regularity in the way terms cancel when expanding $(x - 1)(x + 1)$, $(x - 1)(x^2 + x + 1)$, and $(x - 1)(x^3 + x^2 + x + 1)$ might lead them to the general formula for the sum of a geometric series. As they work to solve a problem, mathematically proficient students maintain oversight of the process, while attending to the details. They continually evaluate the reasonableness of their intermediate results.

Connecting the Standards for Mathematical Practice to the Standards for Mathematical Content

The Standards for Mathematical Practice describe ways in which developing student practitioners of the discipline of mathematics increasingly ought to engage with the subject matter as they grow in mathematical maturity and expertise throughout the elementary, middle and high school years. Designers of curricula, assessments, and professional development should all attend to the need to connect the mathematical practices to mathematical content in mathematics instruction. The Standards for Mathematical Content are a balanced combination of procedure and understanding. Expectations that begin with the word "understand" are often especially good opportunities to connect the practices to the content. Students who lack understanding of a topic may rely on procedures too heavily. Without a flexible base from which to work, they may be less likely to consider analogous problems, represent problems coherently, justify conclusions, apply the mathematics to practical situations, use technology mindfully to work with the mathematics, explain the mathematics accurately to other students, step back for an overview, or deviate from a known procedure to find a shortcut. In short, a lack of understanding effectively prevents a student from engaging in the mathematical practices. In this respect, those content standards which set an expectation of understanding are potential "points of intersection" between the Standards for Mathematical Content and the Standards for Mathematical Practice. These points of intersection are intended to be weighted toward central and generative concepts in the school mathematics curriculum that most merit the time, resources, innovative energies, and focus necessary to qualitatively improve the curriculum, instruction, assessment, professional development, and student achievement in mathematics.

Session 5

Problem Solving With Rational Numbers

Overview

How can problem solving contexts provide opportunities for children to learn new mathematical ideas and gain skills with rational numbers?

Description

Research indicates that problem solving provides an important context in which students can learn about number and other mathematical topics (Kilpatrick, Swafford, & Findell, 2001). It also can provide opportunities for learning new concepts and for practicing learned skills. Students can build understanding of addition and subtraction with decimals through problem solving.

Key Ideas

- Problem solving can serve as a means for students to learn new mathematical ideas and skills.

- Well-crafted problems can inspire children to explore important mathematical ideas, understand various strategies, and learn mathematical relationships.

- It is important to look critically at instructional materials and identify how they support students' understanding of fractions and decimals.

Outline of Activities

- 5.1 Investigating Instructional Materials: Illuminations   (20 minutes)
- 5.2 A Look at Problem Solving   (15 minutes)
- 5.3 A Problem-Solving Task   (25 minutes)

- 5.4 The Problems With Problem Solving   (20 minutes)
- 5.5 Before the Next Session   (5 minutes)
- 5.6 Lesson Design Notes   (5 minutes)

What to Bring

- Notes and student work: NCTM Illuminations activity

To Complete Before Session 6

- Investigating Instructional Materials activity for decimal and fraction connections

Facilitator Notes   Session 5

Problem Solving With Rational Numbers

If this is your first time facilitating the group, please refer to the more detailed facilitator guidelines in the Introduction. As the facilitator, it is generally your job to keep the conversation flowing and watch the clock. Use your judgment to decide when it's appropriate to extend a session for good conversation or when it's time to move on to the next activity. Remember to keep the group norms posted and revise them, as a group, as necessary.

Before the Session

- Make copies of the following handouts for each team member:
    - ☐ 5.3 Problem Solving: The Places on My Street
- Gather the following materials to be used in this session:
    - ☐ Group norms (from Activity 1.4)
    - ☐ Calculators
    - ☐ Base-ten blocks
    - ☐ Centimeter rulers
- Remind team members to bring the following items from previous sessions:
    - ☐ Journal (and writing instruments)
    - ☐ Notes and student work: NCTM Illuminations activity

During the Session

- Post group norms, and revise as a group as necessary.
- Activity 5.1: facilitate discussion; serve as timekeeper.
- Activity 5.2: facilitate discussion.
- Activity 5.3: facilitate discussion and sharing; facilitate partnering, if necessary.
- Activity 5.4: facilitate discussion.

After the Session

- Remind team members of homework, to identify lessons addressing decimal and fraction connections.
- Pass any team materials on to the next facilitator.

Activity 5.1 Investigating Instructional Materials: Illuminations

20 minutes

In this activity, you will report to the group about the NCTM Illuminations lesson that you taught in your classrooms. Identify a timekeeper to make sure that everyone has an opportunity to share.

Before you begin, find out if any of the group members used the same lesson or activity. If so, it may be helpful to combine their reports.

Share how the lesson or activity went and highlights from your reflections. Use student work to illustrate your report. Some common ideas you may want to include are

- Why you selected the lesson or activity

- The goal or learning objective

- Adaptations that you made and why you made them

- Successes and challenges

- Suggestions for other teachers

Discuss any questions that come up with the group.

Activity 5.2 A Look at Problem Solving

15 minutes

In Session 4, you examined the Common Core State Standards for the fourth and fifth grades and spent additional time exploring decimal and fraction concepts.

Read the following excerpt from NCTM's *Principles and Standards for School Mathematics* (2000):

> Problem solving is the cornerstone of school mathematics. Without the ability to solve problems, the usefulness and power of mathematical ideas, knowledge, and skills are severely limited. Students who can efficiently and accurately multiply but who cannot identify situations that call for multiplication are not well prepared . . . Problem solving is also important because it can serve as a vehicle for learning new mathematical ideas and skills . . . Good problems can inspire the exploration of important mathematical ideas, nurture persistence, and reinforce the need to understand and use various strategies, mathematical properties, and relationships. (p. 182)

Discuss the following questions:

- What is your reaction to this excerpt? Is it in alignment or in conflict with the Common Core State Standards? How does it relate to your experience as a mathematical learner and problem solver?

- How can problem solving "serve as a vehicle for learning new mathematical ideas and skills"? What might this look like in a classroom? How could new mathematical ideas and skills about rational numbers be developed through problem solving?

- What successes or challenges do your students have with problem solving?

Activity 5.3 A Problem-Solving Task

25 minutes

Handout 5.3 Problem Solving: The Places on My Street
Base-ten blocks
Calculators
Centimeter rulers

In this activity, you and your team members will work on a problem-solving task using rational numbers.

Read Handout 5.3 Problem Solving: The Places on My Street.

Work with a partner to find the location of each place on Easy Street. Some tools and strategies you might use follow. Challenge yourself to use tools and strategies that you might not typically use in order to build your own mathematical understanding, including approaches that your students might use.

- Using base-ten blocks
- Using a centimeter ruler
- Using drawings or number lines
- Using a calculator
- Using a fractional or decimal benchmark (like 0.5 or $\frac{1}{2}$)
- Using other numerical reasoning or logic

Note: Numerical reasoning includes recognizing relationships among numbers and arithmetic operations, understanding the relative and absolute value of numbers, using referents and benchmarks, composing and decomposing numbers, and estimating.

Discuss the following questions with your group:

- What tools and strategies did you use to find the location of each place? Which tools and strategies were the easiest to use? Which tools and strategies were challenging to use or understand? What tools and strategies might your students use?

- Could this task "serve as a vehicle for learning new mathematical ideas and skills" for students? If this was a teacher's intent, where might it be best placed in the sequence of instruction—at the beginning of a unit on addition and subtraction of decimals, near the middle, or toward the end?

- What manipulatives are available in your classroom for students to access and choose to use as they solve problems?

- Would your students benefit from an activity similar to this? Would they find it challenging? How might you modify this activity to be more appropriate for your students?

Reflect and write in your journal about the important mathematical relationships that came up in your work while finding the location of each place. What concepts and procedures would you want your students to learn? What new ideas do you have about classroom instruction and possible lessons? What questions remain for you about using problem solving to help students learn new mathematical concepts?

Share the ideas you wrote in your journal with your group.

Activity 5.4 The Problems With Problem Solving

20 minutes

Using problem solving as a starting point to build students' understanding of addition and subtraction of rational numbers is the reverse order from a traditional approach to mathematics instruction. It may seem more logical to teach students how to compute with numbers first and save the "harder" problem solving for later in the unit when children are more fluent in operations with decimals and fractions. Teachers often find that helping students solve context-based problems can be one of the most difficult aspects of teaching mathematics.

Discuss the following questions with your group:

- What are your thoughts about the placement of problem solving in a learning sequence? Should problem solving serve as a starting point or should it be an extension to learning, after students develop computational fluency?

- Do you find it difficult to help students become successful with problem solving? What makes this difficult in teaching?

- Generate a list of some of the "problems" or challenges to helping your students become successful problem solvers.

Researchers have done extensive work with teachers who use problem solving to introduce and support students in learning new concepts. Consider the following (simulated) teacher-researcher exchanges. Which of these dialogues relate to the problems or challenges you listed?

❖　　❖　　❖

Teacher: I always found problem solving to be the most difficult part of math. I don't want my students to feel discouraged like I did, so I wait until they have developed confidence with adding, subtracting, multiplying, and dividing with decimals and fractions before posing problems.

Researcher: While many adults struggled with problem solving when they were learning math, this might be precisely because the problems occurred at the end of a unit of study rather than being woven throughout. Research shows that we learn mathematics by making connections, and problem contexts help us to recognize these connections (Kilpatrick et al., 2001; Van de Walle, 2009). When problem solving is the starting place, students can develop broad understanding of all types of problems for finding decimal and fractional amounts. Furthermore, problem solving provides a context that helps children understand what to do in order to find the answer, which leads to fluent computational ability. Developing computational fluency can be enhanced through work with problem solving.

❖ ❖ ❖

Teacher: Problem solving is too complicated for my students. Some of them don't have strong reading skills and when they get to a word problem they get really confused. They can barely handle the simplest problem like 0.5 plus 0.1, how can they possibly solve a problem with all kinds of details to keep track of?

Researcher: Problem solving can and should be posed verbally to students so that reading ability will not be a factor. We often think of problem solving as being more difficult to solve than basic arithmetic problems. The opposite is actually true. Problems that are posed in a familiar situation provide students with an access point for solving them. Rich detail in a problem actually helps students because it allows them to make sense of the situation. When students can associate numerical quantities with particular items and actions in a story, they can make sense of what it means to add, subtract, multiply, or divide. When they are first learning how to operate with decimals and fractions, students benefit from simple and straightforward contexts that help them to conceptualize and model the situation (Kilpatrick et al., 2001).

❖ ❖ ❖

Teacher: Teaching problem solving is too time-consuming. I have a lot of content to cover and I need to make sure all of my students meet standards. If I spend too much time on problem solving, I won't have time to teach them all of the strategies and algorithms they need to know to move ahead.

Researcher: Children who learn mathematics through experiences with problems naturally develop strong problem-solving skills. Without formal or direct instruction on specific algorithms or procedures, children can construct their own solutions to a variety of problems. Children can understand the basic arithmetic operations in terms of their own intuitive problem-solving processes. Symbolic procedures and formal algorithms can be developed as extensions of students' intuitive solution processes (Carpenter, Fennema, Franke, Levi, & Empson, 1999; Cobb et al., 1991).

❖   ❖   ❖

Discuss the following questions with your group:

- Which of these teacher concerns relate to a topic you discussed? What is your reaction to the researchers' responses?
- What problems did you list that were not addressed in these dialogues? How do you think one of these researchers might respond?

Write a response to the following question in your journal:

- What additional questions do you now have about using problem solving to help students learn strategies for mastering decimals and fractions?

Activity 5.5 Before the Next Session

5 minutes

Instructional Materials for Connecting Fractions and Decimals

In Session 7, you will analyze lessons that address the relationship between fractions and decimals. Between now and Session 7, identify a lesson on this topic from your instructional materials. You might select a lesson that you have not taught before, one that you particularly enjoy teaching, or one that is challenging to teach.

The activity in Session 7 will focus on the following questions:

- What big ideas, strategies, and mathematical models are being developed in the lesson?
- What skills and knowledge are required to complete the tasks?
- What are the important mathematical concepts underlying the lesson?
- What are the strengths of the lesson?
- What are some limitations, questions, and concerns that you have about the lesson?

Activity 5.6 Lesson Design Notes

5 minutes

The key ideas for this session are

- Problem solving can serve as a means for students to learn new mathematical ideas and skills.
- Well-crafted problems can inspire children to explore important mathematical ideas, understand various strategies, and learn mathematical relationships.
- It is important to look critically at instructional materials and identify how they support students' understanding of fractions and decimals.

Reflect on what you learned during this session and how the ideas apply to each of the three themes in your Lesson Design Notes. A few prompts related to the themes follow. These are merely suggestions and should not limit your reflection or the ideas you capture.

- Where do you want to go?
  - In Activity 5.3, you examined problem solving as a starting point to build students' understanding of rational numbers. What are your goals for students in the area of problem solving?
- Where are you now?
  - In Activity 5.1, you shared the NCTM Illuminations lesson you taught. How did your students respond to the lesson? What did they already understand? What concepts did they find more of a struggle?
- What is the best way to get there?
  - From the discussion on the NCTM Illuminations lesson, what ideas about instruction did you learn from the group? Which of these ideas would you like to try out in your classroom? How might these instructional strategies help your students learn important ideas about rational numbers?

References and Resources

Carpenter, T. P., Fennema, E., Franke, M. L., Levi, L., & Empson, S. B. (1999). *Children's mathematics: Cognitively guided instruction.* Portsmouth, NH: Heinemann.

Cobb, P., Wood, T., Yackel, E., Nichills, J., Wheatley, G., Trigatti, B., & Perlwitz, M. (1991). Assessment of a problem-centered second-grade mathematics project. *Journal for Research in Mathematics Education, 22,* 3–29.

Kilpatrick, J., Swafford, J., & Findell, B. (Eds.). (2001). *Adding it up: Helping children learn mathematics.* Washington, DC: National Academies Press.

National Council of Teachers of Mathematics (2000). *Principles and standards for school mathematics.* Reston, VA: National Council of Teachers of Mathematics.

Van de Walle, J. A. (2009). *Elementary and middle school mathematics: Teaching developmentally* (7th ed.). Needham Heights, MA: Allyn & Bacon.

Handout 5.3
Problem Solving: The Places on My Street

I live on Easy Street. It's not really called that, but it's the way I think of it because most of the places I need to go are on my street. In fact, they are all located in the one-mile strip between Beech Street and Elm Street. If we start at Beech Street, I'd walk the following distances to each location, from the corner of Easy and Beech:

Place	Beech	Grocery Store	Library	Park	Elm
Distance (miles)	0	0.27	0.8	0.95	1

Oops! I left out a few locations: school, the doctor's office, the fire station, the police station, and my house. Let's see if you can find them with these clues:

- ☐ The school is half the distance from Beech to Elm.
- ☐ The library (where my dad works) and the fire station (where my mom works) are the same distance from the school.
- ☐ It is farther to the park from the fire station than it is from the library.
- ☐ The doctor's office and the police station are 0.05 miles apart, as are the doctor's office and the fire station.
- ☐ The grocery store is closer to the fire station than to the police station.
- ☐ From my house, I could walk to the library and back in the same time it would take me to get to the park. This is twice the time it would take me to walk to school from my house.
- ☐ From my house, it takes me a little longer to walk to the grocery store than it takes me to walk all the way to Elm Street.

Where do I live?

Session 6

Decimal and Fraction Relationships

Overview

How can teachers build on children's existing knowledge of fractions to learn decimals and identify important mathematical relationships between fractions and decimals?

Description

Fractions with denominators that are powers of 10 (such as $\frac{3}{10}$, $\frac{60}{100}$, and $\frac{125}{1,000}$) can serve as a bridge to connect students' fraction understanding with their decimal knowledge. Emphasizing the numerical relationships between fractions and decimals will allow students to draw upon their understanding of both fractions and decimals and develop a deep and flexible understanding of rational numbers.

Key Ideas

- Drawing upon students' existing knowledge of fractions will support their learning and understanding of decimal numbers.

- Base-ten blocks can help students develop an understanding of the relationship between fractions and decimals.

- Children with a deep understanding of rational numbers will develop flexible and efficient strategies for finding fraction and decimal equivalents that include numerical reasoning.

Outline of Activities

- 6.1 Connecting Fractions and Decimals   (30 minutes)
- 6.2 Finding Decimal Equivalents for Fractions (30 minutes)
- 6.3 Defining Mathematical Proficiency   (20 minutes)
- 6.4 Before the Next Session   (5 minutes)
- 6.5 Lesson Design Notes   (5 minutes)

To Complete Before Session 7

- Student Connections: Equivalent Fractions and Decimals (Handout 6.4)

Facilitator Notes   Session 6

Decimal and Fraction Relationships

If this is your first time facilitating the group, please refer to the more detailed facilitator guidelines in the Introduction. As the facilitator, it is generally your job to keep the conversation flowing and watch the clock. Use your judgment to decide when it's appropriate to extend a session for good conversation or when it's time to move on to the next activity. Remember to keep the group norms posted and revise them, as a group, as necessary.

Before the Session

- Make copies of the following handouts for each team member:
    - ☐ 6.1 Base-Ten Fractions
    - ☐ 6.2 Fractions to Decimals
    - ☐ 6.3 Five Strands of Mathematical Proficiency
    - ☐ 6.4 Student Connections: Equivalent Fractions and Decimals
- Gather the following materials to be used in this session:
    - ☐ Group norms (from Activity 1.4)
    - ☐ Chart paper and markers
    - ☐ Base-ten blocks (thousand cubes, hundred flats, ten sticks, and unit cubes)
    - ☐ Calculators
    - ☐ Ten-by-ten grids (or graph paper)
- Remind team members to bring the following items from previous sessions:
    - ☐ Journal (and writing instruments)

During the Session

- Post group norms, and revise as a group as necessary.
- Activity 6.1: facilitate discussion and sharing; facilitate partnering, as necessary.
- Activity 6.2: facilitate discussion and sharing.
- Activity 6.3: facilitate partnering, as necessary; serve as recorder.
- Activity 6.4: facilitate partnering, if necessary.

After the Session

- Remind team members of homework, to identify lessons addressing decimal and fraction connections, and Handout 6.4 Student Connections: Equivalent Fractions and Decimals.
- Pass any team materials on to the next facilitator.

Activity 6.1 Connecting Fractions and Decimals

30 minutes

Handout 6.1 Base-Ten Fractions
Base-ten blocks: thousand cubes,
hundred flats, ten sticks, and unit cubes

Decimals are a way of writing fractions using base-ten equivalents. For example, 0.45 is another way of writing $^{45}/_{100}$. The big ideas and important concepts pertaining to fractions also apply to decimals. *Decimal fractions* or *base-ten fractions* are fractions with denominators that are powers of 10 (10, 100, 1000). They can serve as a bridge connecting students' fraction understanding with their decimal knowledge (Baroody, 1998). When instruction emphasizes the connection between decimals and fractions, students can integrate their knowledge of rational numbers into a unified whole. Seeing and using connections between fractions and decimals helps students build proficiency with both.

Baroody's (1998) *Fostering Children's Mathematical Power: An Investigative Approach to K–8 Mathematics Instruction* provides the following suggestion:

> To foster an understanding of decimals, teachers can help children see (a) the connection between fractions and decimals and (b) the connection between decimals and base-ten, place-value concepts. Instruction should proceed from fractions to decimal fractions (e.g., $^{1}/_{10}$, $^{5}/_{10}$, $^{17}/_{100}$, $^{27}/_{1,000}$) and then to decimals. (p. 11–4)

Discuss the following questions:

- Is the instructional sequence recommended here (from fractions to decimal fractions and then to decimals) the one you typically follow for these concepts? If so, do you agree with the researchers that this is a productive way to build student understanding? If not, what potential benefits can you see in this sequence?

- To what degree do your instructional materials emphasize the connection among fractions, decimal fractions, and decimals? What could you do to strengthen these connections?

The use of models can be an effective way to help students make connections among fractions, decimal fractions, and decimals (Fosnot & Dolk, 2002). The following activity provides an example of an instructional task that connects decimal fractions with decimal numbers using base-ten blocks as the model.

Read and solve the questions on Handout 6.1 Base-Ten Fractions with a partner. As you work, consider how your students would solve the problem.

Discuss the following questions:

- How did you solve each of the problems on Handout 6.1? How did your solution strategy make use of the mathematical relationship among ones, tenths, hundredths, and thousandths? How did your solution strategy make use of the relationship between fractions and decimals?

- How do you think your students would solve these problems? Would the base-ten model support or limit their understanding of the relationship between fractions and decimals? How? What other models might also be helpful?

- What types of learning experiences can you provide for students to strengthen their understanding of the relationship between fractions and decimals?

Write in your journal about how you can adapt and extend the use of this model, base-ten blocks, to help your students identify connections among fractions, decimal fractions, and decimal numbers. When you are finished writing, share your ideas with others in your group.

Activity 6.2 Finding Decimal Equivalents for Fractions

30 minutes   Handout 6.2 Fractions to Decimals
                                    Calculators, base-ten blocks, and ten-by-ten grids

Decimals and fractions can be challenging for many students to learn. The National Research Council states in *Adding It Up* (Kilpatrick, Swofford, & Kindell, 2001), "Learning about rational numbers is more complicated and difficult than learning about whole numbers. Rational numbers are more complex than whole numbers, in part because they are represented in several ways (e.g., common fractions [fractions in which both the numerator and denominator are integers] and decimal fractions) and used in many ways (e.g., as parts of regions and sets, as ratios, as quotients)" (p. 231). As you discussed in the previous activity, building on students' knowledge of fractions to include decimal fractions, or base-ten fractions, and then decimal numbers will help students see connections among these multiple representations and identify the important relationships among them.

Read Handout 6.2 Fractions to Decimals.

Work with a partner to find fraction and decimal equivalents. Use *at least two* approaches to justify each one, including approaches that your students might use. A list of tools and strategies you might use follows. Challenge yourself to use tools and strategies that you might not typically use in order to build your own mathematical understanding.

- Using base-ten blocks
- Using ten-by-ten grids
- Using a calculator
- Using numerical reasoning
- Using another decimal value that you already know
- Using long division

Discuss the following questions with your group:

- Which tools and strategies did you use to find equivalent decimals? Which tools and strategies were the easiest to use? Which tools and strategies were challenging to use or understand? Why and how does each strategy work?

- What patterns and relationships do you see among the fractions and decimals? What patterns and relationships might your students see? What patterns and relationships will you look for in student work?

- How are the decimal equivalents for halves, fourths, fifths, eighths, and tenths different from those of thirds, sixths, and ninths? Why do the decimal equivalents for thirds, sixths, and ninths repeat? How would you represent decimal equivalents for thirds, sixths, and ninths using base-ten blocks and ten-by-ten grids? How would you find these equivalents using long division or a calculator?

- How did the experience of using two approaches for each reinforce connections between fractions and decimals? For example, in what way is the use of base-ten blocks connected to the keys pressed when using a calculator?

- Would your students benefit from an activity similar to this? How might you modify this activity to be more appropriate for fourth or fifth graders?

Reflect and write in your journal about the important mathematical relationships that came up in your work with finding equivalent fractions and decimals. What concepts would you want your students to understand? What new ideas do you have about classroom instruction and possible lessons? What questions remain for you about equivalent fractions and decimals and student learning?

Share the ideas you wrote in your journal with your group.

Activity 6.3 Defining Mathematical Proficiency

20 minutes   Handout 6.3 Five Strands of Mathematical Proficiency

Now we will take an in-depth look at instructional goals. While we often think of goals in terms of specific concepts and processes to be accomplished in a single lesson, it is also helpful to step back and consider the bigger picture. Each lesson is a step in a journey that moves your students toward success in their mathematical careers. For this reason, when planning individual lessons, teachers should also be mindful of their long-term goals for their students. To define and discuss long-term mathematical goals, we will consider what it means to be mathematically proficient.

Brainstorm individually in your journal about a student you have known whom you consider to be mathematically proficient. Write the name of that student at the top of the page. Now make a list of the qualities or characteristics that distinguish this student from others whom you did not consider to be as mathematically proficient.

- What could the student do that others could not do?

- What kinds of things did the student say that revealed deep mathematical understanding?

- What were the visible attributes that led you to conclude that the student was mathematically proficient?

Also consider an adult you have known whom you consider to be mathematically proficient. Add the qualities and characteristics of this person to your list.

- What has the adult said or done that makes you believe this individual is mathematically proficient?
- What are the visible attributes that led you to conclude that this adult is mathematically proficient?

Share your list with a partner. Identify four or five qualities or characteristics that you and your partner agree are important descriptions that apply to both adults and children who are mathematically proficient.

Share the four or five qualities you and your partner listed with the group. Keep a running group list on chart paper. If a quality is mentioned by more than one partner pair, put a star next to it.

Read Handout 6.3. This handout summarizes a definition of mathematical proficiency developed by the National Research Council (NRC). The NRC has described mathematical proficiency as being composed of five interconnected strands: conceptual understanding, procedural fluency, strategic competence, adaptive reasoning, and productive disposition.

Compare your group's statements recorded on the chart paper with the list on Handout 6.3.

- Which of the NRC strands are represented by qualities you have written on your list?
- Are there any statements on your chart paper that do not match any of the strands?
- Are there any strands for which you did not generate any statements?

Write in your journal about how the five strands relate to your students.

- Which of the five strands is strongly evident in many of your students? Name a few of these students.
- Which of the five strands is not particularly evident in many of your students? Why do you think this is so?

Activity 6.4 Before the Next Session

5 minutes   Handout 6.4 Student Connections: Equivalent Fractions and Decimals

Student Connections

Before the next session, pose the problems on Handout 6.4 to several of your students. Take a few minutes right now to solve each of the problems with a partner and talk about possible solutions that students may come up with.

Choose three students of varied ability levels. Sit with students individually as they complete the task and record what they say and do in your journal. Try to be as detailed as possible in describing how they approach the task, how difficult the task is for your students, what errors they make, and anything else of interest that happens during the interview. The purpose of this and other Student Connections activities is for you to collect some data about your students that will be shared at the next meeting. Using your students' responses and notes in your journal, be prepared to report back next time on students' understanding of finding decimal equivalents for fractions and fraction equivalents for decimals.

Activity 6.5 Lesson Design Notes

5 minutes

The key ideas for this session are

- Drawing upon students' existing knowledge of fractions will support their learning and understanding of decimal numbers.
- Base-ten blocks can help students develop an understanding of the relationship between fractions and decimals.
- Children with a deep understanding of rational numbers will develop flexible and efficient strategies for finding fraction and decimal equivalents that include numerical reasoning.

Reflect on what you learned during this session and how the ideas apply to each of the three themes in your Lesson Design Notes. A few prompts related to the themes follow. These are merely suggestions and should not limit your reflection or the ideas you capture.

- Where do you want to go?
  - o In Activity 6.3, you discussed mathematical proficiency. Which of the five strands of mathematical proficiency would you like to explore further and help your students develop?
- Where are you now?
  - o How can the five strands of mathematical proficiency help you determine where your students are now?
- What is the best way to get there?
  - o In Activity 6.1, you explored the connection between decimal fractions (or base-ten fractions) with decimal numbers. How can the examination of this relationship help students build a deeper understanding of fractions and decimals?

References and Resources

Baroody, A. J. (with Coslick, R.T.). (1998). *Fostering children's mathematical power: An investigative approach to K–8 mathematics instruction.* Mahwah, NJ: Lawrence Erlbaum.

Fosnot, C. T., & Dolk, M. (2002). *Young mathematicians at work: Constructing fractions, decimals and percents.* Portsmouth, NH: Heinemann.

Kilpatrick, J., Swafford, J., & Findell, B. (Eds.). (2001). *Adding it up: Helping children learn mathematics.* Washington, DC: National Academies Press.

Handout 6.1
Base-Ten Fractions

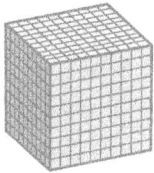

For this activity, the large cube has a value of one.

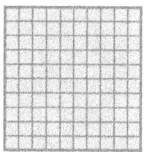

Flat   Rod   Small cube

1. What fraction and decimal show the value of the flat?

                                          Fraction   Decimal

2. What fraction and decimal show the value of the rod?

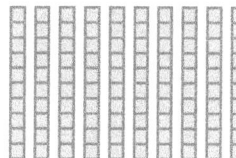

                                            Fraction   Decimal

3. What fraction and decimal show the value of the small cube?

                                            Fraction   Decimal

4. Are the fraction and decimal that show the value of a flat [image] equivalent to the

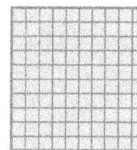

fraction and decimal that show the value of ten rods [image] ?
Why or why not? Explain your thinking.

5. What fraction and decimal show the value of [image] ?

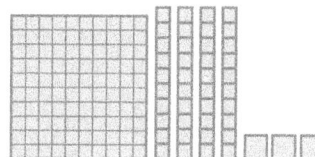

6. Build a model for $\frac{235}{1,000}$ using base-ten blocks. What is the equivalent decimal?

Handout 6.2
Fractions to Decimals

$\frac{1}{2} =$	$\frac{1}{3} =$	$\frac{1}{4} =$	$\frac{1}{5} =$	$\frac{1}{6} =$	$\frac{1}{8} =$	$\frac{1}{9} =$	$\frac{1}{10} =$
$\frac{2}{2} =$	$\frac{2}{3} =$	$\frac{2}{4} =$	$\frac{2}{5} =$	$\frac{2}{6} =$	$\frac{2}{8} =$	$\frac{2}{9} =$	$\frac{2}{10} =$
	$\frac{3}{3} =$	$\frac{3}{4} =$	$\frac{3}{5} =$	$\frac{3}{6} =$	$\frac{3}{8} =$	$\frac{3}{9} =$	$\frac{3}{10} =$
		$\frac{4}{4} =$	$\frac{4}{5} =$	$\frac{4}{6} =$	$\frac{4}{8} =$	$\frac{4}{9} =$	$\frac{4}{10} =$
			$\frac{5}{5} =$	$\frac{5}{6} =$	$\frac{5}{8} =$	$\frac{5}{9} =$	$\frac{5}{10} =$
				$\frac{6}{6} =$	$\frac{6}{8} =$	$\frac{6}{9} =$	$\frac{6}{10} =$
					$\frac{7}{8} =$	$\frac{7}{9} =$	$\frac{7}{10} =$
					$\frac{8}{8} =$	$\frac{8}{9} =$	$\frac{8}{10} =$
						$\frac{9}{9} =$	$\frac{9}{10} =$
							$\frac{10}{10} =$

Handout 6.3
Five Strands of Mathematical Proficiency

In the past, students in elementary school were considered successful when they had memorized procedures well enough to complete many simple problems in a short amount of time. The growing knowledge about how people learn makes it clear that memorizing procedures is not the same as learning mathematics with understanding and being able to think mathematically. Mathematical proficiency is the key to being able to apply mathematics to unfamiliar and complex situations.

The National Research Council (Kilpatrick, Swafford, & Findell, 2001) has proposed a comprehensive definition of mathematical proficiency, made up of five components or strands. These five strands are intertwined, meaning that they do not exist in isolation but are interrelated.

1. *Conceptual understanding:* Mathematically proficient students understand mathematical concepts, operations, and relations. They know what mathematical symbols, diagrams, and procedures mean.

2. *Procedural fluency:* Mathematically proficient students carry out mathematical procedures—such as adding, subtracting, multiplying, and dividing numbers—flexibly, accurately, efficiently, and appropriately.

3. *Strategic competence:* Mathematically proficient students are able to formulate problems mathematically and to devise strategies for solving them by using concepts and procedures appropriately.

4. *Adaptive reasoning:* Mathematically proficient students use logic to explain and justify a solution to a problem or to extend from something known to something not yet known.

5. *Productive disposition:* Mathematically proficient students see mathematics as sensible, useful, and doable—*and* they are willing to work at it.

Source: J. Kilpatrick, J. Swafford, & B. Findell (Eds.). (2001). *Adding it up: Helping children learn mathematics.* Washington, DC: National Academies Press.

Handout 6.4

Student Connections: Equivalent Fractions and Decimals

Name:

What is a decimal that is equivalent to $\frac{2}{5}$? Explain why they are equal using words, numbers, and pictures.

What is a fraction that is equivalent to 0.75? Explain why they are equal using words, numbers, and pictures.

Write a fraction and decimal that are equivalent. Explain why they are equal using words, numbers, and pictures.

_____ = _____

The decimal 0.15 and the fraction $\frac{1}{5}$ both use the same numbers. Explain why they are *not* equal to each other using words, numbers, and pictures.

Session 7

Comparing and Ordering Decimals and Fractions

Overview

How can mathematical games help students develop reasoning skills for comparing decimals and fractions?

Description

Building flexibility and fluency with rational numbers requires that students develop a strong understanding of the numerical relationships between fractions and decimals. It is important for students to have multiple opportunities to practice comparing decimals and fractions. Mathematics games can provide engaging contexts for skill practice and strategic thinking.

Key Ideas

- Mathematics games provide opportunities for students to practice comparing and ordering decimals and fractions in an engaging context.
- Instruction that invites students to develop multiple strategies to compare and order decimals and fractions, supported by important mathematical concepts, helps develop number sense.

Outline of Activities

- 7.1 Analyzing Student Connections   (15 minutes)
- 7.2 Mathematics Games   (45 minutes)
- 7.3 Investigating Instructional Materials: (20 minutes)
  Connecting Fractions and Decimals
- 7.4 Before the Next Session   (5 minutes)
- 7.5 Lesson Design Notes   (5 minutes)

What to Bring

- Notes and student work: Student Connections (Handout 6.4)
- Instructional materials: lessons addressing decimal and fraction connections
- Handout 4.4 from previous sessions
- Common Core State Standards: Standards for Mathematical Content

To Complete Before Session 8

- Student Connections: Fraction and Decimal Games (Handout 7.4)

Facilitator Notes   Session 7

Comparing and Ordering Decimals and Fractions

If this is your first time facilitating the group, please refer to the more detailed facilitator guidelines in the Introduction. As the facilitator, it is generally your job to keep the conversation flowing and watch the clock. Use your judgment to decide when it's appropriate to extend a session for good conversation or when it's time to move on to the next activity. Remember to keep the group norms posted and revise them, as a group, as necessary.

Before the Session

- Make copies of the following handouts for each team member:
  - ☐ 7.2A Mathematics Games: Comparing and Ordering Decimals and Fractions
  - ☐ 7.2B Game Cards: Decimals and Fractions
  - ☐ 7.2C Match Cards
  - ☐ 7.2D Greater Than One-Half Game Board
  - ☐ 7.3A Sample Lesson: Fourth Grade
  - ☐ 7.3B Sample Lesson: Fifth Grade
  - ☐ 7.3C Investigating Instructional Materials: Fourth Grade Lesson
  - ☐ 7.3D Investigating Instructional Materials: Fifth Grade Lesson
  - ☐ 7.3E Investigating Your Instructional Materials: Analyzing Lessons
  - ☐ 7.4 Student Connections: Fraction and Decimal Games
- Gather the following materials to be used in this session:
  - ☐ Group norms (from Activity 1.4)
  - ☐ Prepare card sets (Handouts 7.2B and 7.2C) on two colors of card stock (see Handout 7.2A)
  - ☐ Scissors
- Remind team members to bring the following items from previous sessions:
  - ☐ Journal (and writing instruments)
  - ☐ Handout 4.4 Common Core State Standards
  - ☐ Common Core State Standards: Standards for Mathematical Content
  - ☐ Completed homework, Identifying Instructional Materials activity connecting fractions and decimals, and completed Handout 6.4 Student Connections: Equivalent Fractions and Decimals

During the Session

- Post group norms, and revise as a group as necessary.
- Activity 7.1: facilitate discussion.

- Activity 7.2: facilitate discussion and sharing; facilitate partnering, if necessary.
- Activity 7.3: facilitate discussion; facilitate partnering, if necessary.

After the Session

- Remind team members of homework, Handout 7.4 Student Connections: Fraction and Decimal Games.
- Pass any team materials on to the next facilitator.

Activity 7.1 Analyzing Student Connections

15 minutes   Handout 6.4 Student Connections: Equivalent Fractions and Decimals

Your task from the last session was to pose the problems from Handout 6.4 to several of your students. You were to ask students to explain why a given fraction and decimal are equivalent using words, numbers, and pictures.

Share your results with your group, using the following questions:

- What pictures or models did your students use in their explanations? How did each model represent the equivalent and nonequivalent values?

- Numerical reasoning includes recognizing relationships among numbers and arithmetic operations, understanding the relative and absolute value of numbers, using referents and benchmarks, composing and decomposing numbers, and estimating. Did some students use numerical reasoning to find equivalent fractions and decimals? Did their reasoning lead to a correct solution or were there misconceptions in their thinking?

- For the last problem, describe the explanations students provided for why the given fraction and decimal are *not* equivalent. Were the explanations supported by numerical reasoning and appropriate models or pictures?

Reflect on your students' numerical reasoning and use of models for finding equivalent fractions. How will you use this information to guide your instruction? As a teacher, what would be possible next steps for you to take with students who have similar levels of understanding for identifying equivalent fractions?

Record your ideas in your journal.

Activity 7.2 Mathematics Games

45 minutes   Handout 7.2A Mathematics Games: Comparing and Ordering Decimals and Fractions
Handout 7.2B Game Cards: Decimals and Fractions
Handout 7.2C Match Cards
Handout 7.2D Greater Than One-Half Game Board

Games provide an opportunity for students to practice mathematical procedures in an engaging, interactive setting. The games you will examine in this activity—Capture Decimals and Fractions, Monkey in the Middle, Greater Than One-Half, and Match—are games that require players to compare and order decimals and fractions.

Read the descriptions of the four games on Handout 7.2A.

Play each game with a partner.

Discuss each game with your partner, using the following questions:

- How could each game help students develop understanding of the relationship between decimals and fractions?
- How does each game help students to develop flexible strategies for comparing and ordering decimals and fractions? Are there any strategies that you would like to add to your learning landscape?
- What variations to the rules or structure of the games could you use that would make the games more or less challenging for some of your students?

Share your partner discussion with the group.

Activity 7.3 Investigating Instructional Materials: Connecting Fractions and Decimals

20 minutes

Handout 4.4 Common Core State Standards

Handout 7.3A Sample Lesson: Fourth Grade

Handout 7.3B Sample Lesson: Fifth Grade

Handout 7.3C Investigating Instructional Materials: Fourth Grade Lesson

Handout 7.3D Investigating Instructional Materials: Fifth Grade Lesson

Handout 7.3E Investigating Your Instructional Materials: Analyzing Lessons

Instructional Materials: lessons connecting fractions and decimals

Common Core State Standards: Standards for Mathematical Content

At several points in the *Teaching by Design* sessions, you will look at sample instructional materials. The goal in providing lessons or activities from different instructional programs is to give you a range of examples to consider when working on your prototype lesson. None of the sample lessons is intended as an exemplar, but simply to demonstrate one way textbook authors have chosen to address the topic.

Review the sample lesson for your grade level on Handout 7.3A or 7.3B with a partner.

Try some of the lesson activities. Look closely at the lesson and consider the questions that follow. Handouts 7.3C and 7.3D list the same questions in a table where you can record your responses.

- What big ideas, strategies, and mathematical models are being developed in the lesson? (See Handout 2.3 in your journal.)
- What are the important mathematical concepts underlying the lesson? How does the lesson reflect the concepts from the Common Core State Standards? (See Handout 4.4 and Standards for Mathematical Content for your grade level.)
- What skills and knowledge are required to complete the tasks?

- For the fourth grade lesson, discuss the following questions:
  - What are the benefits of using base-ten blocks to represent the value of fractions and decimals? What does the model help students see or understand about the relationship between fractions and decimals?
  - This lesson includes a sample class discussion. How does the teacher facilitate a discussion on the relationship between equivalent fractions and decimals? How does the teacher make connections between the model (base-ten blocks) and symbolic representations (equations)?
- For the fifth grade lesson, discuss the following questions:
  - What are the benefits of using the number line to represent the value of fractions and decimals? What does the model help students see or understand about the relationship between fractions and decimals?
  - The lesson asks students to identify pairs of number cards that show equalities and inequalities, and then asks for an explanation of why they think the pairs are either equal or unequal. How might your students justify whether or not pairs of number cards are either equal or unequal? What types of reasoning might they use?
- What are the strengths of the lesson?
- What are some limitations, questions, and concerns that you have about the lesson?

Repeat the process above with a lesson from your own curriculum. In your homework from Session 5, you may have selected a lesson for analysis that focuses on the same topic or concepts as the sample lesson. You can analyze the same lesson as a group or work individually on different lessons. Handout 7.3E includes a table similar to the one from Handouts 7.3C and 7.3D and should be used to record your observations about the lesson from your curriculum.

Discuss responses on both handouts as a group. What portions of these lessons might you combine to make the learning experience stronger for your students?

Activity 7.4 Before the Next Session

5 minutes   Handout 7.2A Mathematics Games: Comparing and Ordering Decimals and Fractions
                          Handout 7.4 Student Connections: Fraction and Decimal Games
                                  Cards and game boards (see Handouts 7.2B, 7.2C, and 7.2D)

Before the next session, select one of the games from Activity 7.2 to play with a small group of students. Sit with the group as they play the game and record what each student says and does. Record your observations on Handout 7.4. Try to be as detailed as possible in describing how each student approaches the games, the strategies they use, what errors they make, and anything else of interest that happens during the observation.

Write in your journal about what you learned about student thinking while observing the students playing these games. What approaches did they use? Was there anything that surprised you? How will you use this information to design learning experiences for your students on comparing and ordering fractions and decimals?

Activity 7.5 Lesson Design Notes

5 minutes

The key ideas for this session are

- Mathematics games provide opportunities for students to practice comparing and ordering decimals and fractions in an engaging context.
- Instruction that invites students to develop multiple strategies to compare and order decimals and fractions, supported by important mathematical concepts, helps develop number sense.

Reflect on what you learned during this session and how the ideas apply to each of the three themes in your Lesson Design Notes. A few prompts related to the themes follow. These are merely suggestions and should not limit your reflection or the ideas you capture.

- Where do you want to go?
  - In Activity 7.2, you played several games and discussed the flexible strategies that can be developed through these games. Which of these strategies would you like your students to learn?

- Where are you now?
  - In Activity 7.1, you examined students' approaches for finding equivalent fractions and decimals. What did you learn about your students' understanding of fractions and decimals?

- What is the best way to get there?
  - In Activity 7.4, you analyzed sample lessons. What ideas from the sample lessons are you interested in trying out in your classroom?

References and Resources

Barnett, C., Goldenstein, D., & Jackson, B. (Eds.). (1994). *Fractions, decimals, ratios, and percents: Hard to teach and hard to learn?* Portsmouth, NH: Heinemann.

Baroody, A. J. (with Coslick, R. T.). (1998). *Fostering children's mathematical power: An investigative approach to K–8 mathematics instruction.* Mahwah, NJ: Lawrence Erlbaum.

Clemson University, & Carolina Biological Supply Company. (2009). *Developing number concepts: Values and variables. Math out of the box: Grade 5.* Burlington, NC: Carolina Biological Supply Company.

Deerwater, R., Fischer, A. E., & Fisher, A. (2007). *Bridges in Mathematics: Grade 4, Teachers Guide* (Vol. 3). Salem, OR: The Math Learning Center.

Fosnot, C. T., & Dolk, M. (2002). Young mathematicians at work: Constructing fractions, decimals and percents. Portsmouth, NH: Heinemann.

Lamon, S. J. (1999). *Teaching fractions and ratios for understanding.* Mahwah, NJ: Lawrence Erlbaum.

Van de Walle, J. A. (2009). *Elementary and middle school mathematics: Teaching developmentally* (7th ed.). Needham Heights, MA: Allyn & Bacon.

Mathematics Games: Comparing and Ordering Decimals and Fractions

Capture Decimals and Fractions

Materials: Handout 7.2B Cards for Capture Decimals and Fractions, and one deck of cards prepared for each pair of players by copying the decimal numbers sheet on cardstock using one color and the fractions sheet on cardstock using a second color

Groups: To be played in pairs

Directions:

- One player gets the fraction cards and the other player gets the decimal cards. Players each shuffle their own cards and keep the deck facedown in one pile.
- To play a round, players each turn over one card from the top of their own deck.
- The player with the largest value gets to keep both cards and places these cards faceup in that player's own separate "captured" pile.
- Players must discuss and verify the relative value of the cards.
- If the two players have cards of equal value, they each lay down another card.
- The one with the largest value keeps all of the cards that have been laid down.
- Play continues until players run out of cards.
- The player who captures the most cards wins.

❖ ❖ ❖

Monkey in the Middle

Materials: Handout 7.2B Cards for Monkey in the Middle, and one deck of cards prepared on cardstock

Groups: Three players or five players

Directions:

- One player deals all the cards (with the fractions and decimals mixed) equally among the players. Players each shuffle their own cards and keep them facedown in one pile.
- To play a round, players each turn over one card from the top of their deck.
- All players work together to place the cards in numerical order from least to greatest. The player with the card whose value is between the other two, "the monkey in the middle," gets to keep all of the cards.
- If two cards happen to share the middle value, then those two players share the cards equally with the extra card placed in a discard pile.
- Play continues until all players run out of cards.
- The player who captures the most cards wins.

❖ ❖ ❖

Greater Than One-Half

Materials: Handout 7.2B Cards for Greater Than One-Half, one deck of cards prepared on cardstock, and Handout 7.2D Greater Than One-Half Game Board for each player

Groups: Two to four players

Directions:

- One player shuffles all of the cards (fractions and decimals together) and places the deck facedown in one pile.
- Players take turns getting a card from the top of the pile and determining whether or not it is less than, greater than, or equal to one-half. Players each place their card along the correct place on their individual game board.
- All players verify the correct placement of each card based on whether or not it is less than, greater than, or equal to one-half.
- Play continues until there are no more cards in the pile.
- The player with the most cards greater than one-half on that player's game board wins.

Variations:

- The player with the most cards that are less than one-half wins.
- The player with the most cards equal to one-half wins.
- Change the value of one-half on the game board to another number between 0 and 1, such as $\frac{1}{3}$ or $\frac{3}{4}$.

❖ ❖ ❖

Match

Materials: Handout 7.2C Match Cards, copied onto cardstock and cut along the lines

Groups: Two players

Directions:

- Cards are shuffled and placed facedown in a four-by-five array.
- Players take turns turning over two cards and looking for a pair of cards that are equivalent. If a match is found, the player keeps the pair of cards. If a match is not found, the cards remain faceup.
- The next player turns over two new cards and may find a match using any of the faceup cards.
- Players each explain how they figured out the numbers are equivalent before taking the pair of cards and placing it in their own pile.
- The player with the most cards at the end wins the game.

Cards: Capture Decimals and Fractions, Monkey in the Middle, and Greater Than One-Half

$\dfrac{1}{2}$	$\dfrac{1}{4}$	$\dfrac{2}{4}$	$\dfrac{3}{4}$
$\dfrac{1}{5}$	$\dfrac{2}{5}$	$\dfrac{3}{5}$	$\dfrac{4}{5}$
$\dfrac{1}{8}$	$\dfrac{2}{8}$	$\dfrac{3}{8}$	$\dfrac{4}{8}$
$\dfrac{5}{8}$	$\dfrac{6}{8}$	$\dfrac{7}{8}$	$\dfrac{3}{10}$
$\dfrac{40}{100}$	$\dfrac{50}{100}$	$\dfrac{8}{100}$	$\dfrac{3}{100}$

.5	.25	.50	.75
.2	.4	.6	.8
.125	.25	.375	.05
.625	.725	.875	.3
.40	.55	.08	.03

Handout 7.2C
Match Cards

$\dfrac{1}{100}$	.01	$\dfrac{1}{2}$	.5
$\dfrac{7}{10}$	.70	$\dfrac{5}{100}$	.05
$\dfrac{1}{4}$	.250	$\dfrac{1}{8}$	.125
.1400	.14	$\dfrac{5}{8}$	.625
.025	$\dfrac{1}{40}$	$\dfrac{1}{10}$	.10

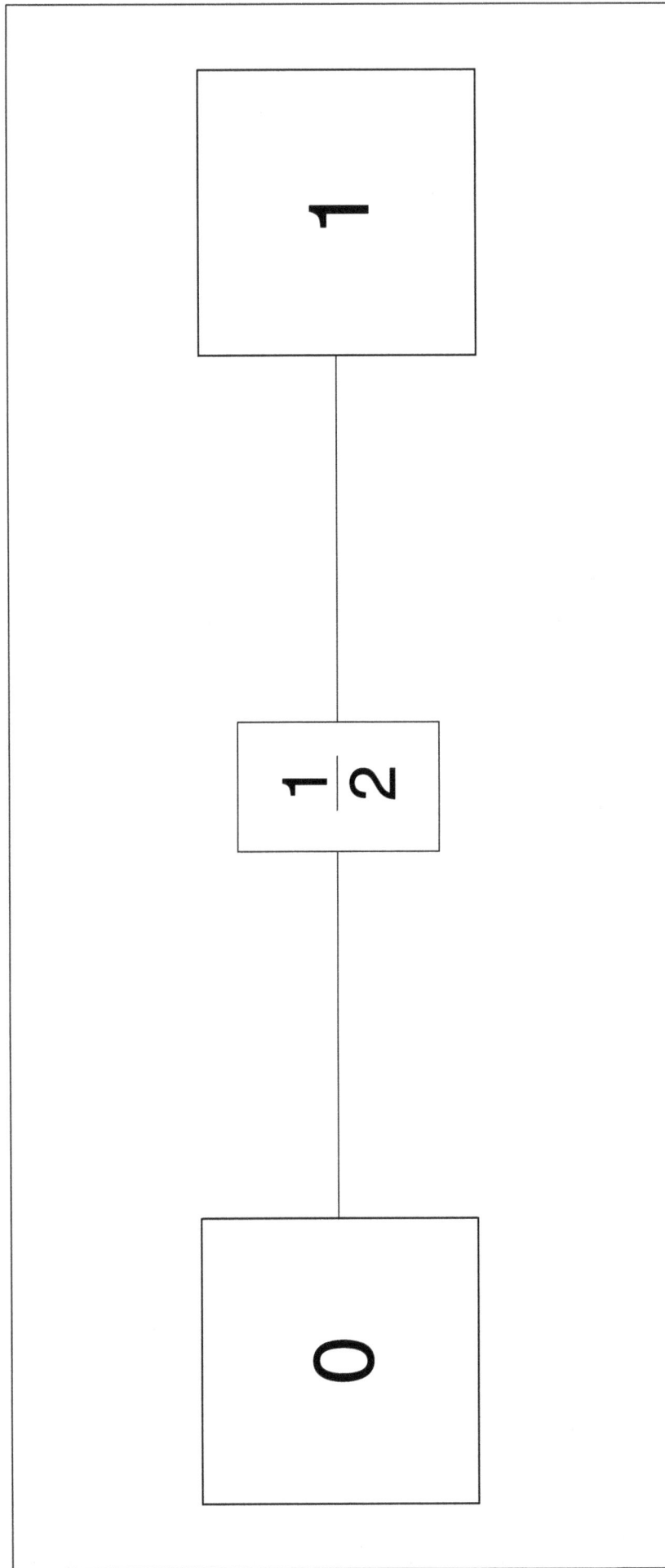

Greater Than One-Half Game Board

0	$\dfrac{1}{2}$	1

Handout 7.3A
Sample Lesson: Fourth Grade

Session 13

HOME
CONNECTIONS

WORK
SAMPLE

Decimal & Fraction Relationships

Overview
Students investigate the relationships between fractions and decimals by modeling various fractions with base ten pieces and then naming them as decimals. At the end of the session, the teacher assigns Home Connection 46, which reinforces the connection between fractions and decimals.

Actions
1. Students explore the relationship between tenths and fifths.

2. Students work independently or in pairs to investigate more decimal and fraction relationships.

3. The teacher introduces Home Connection 46, Decimals Are Fractions.

Skills & Concepts
★ relating decimals to fractions using concrete models of tenths and hundredths, such as money and base ten number pieces

★ recognizing, modeling, ordering, comparing, and using decimals to hundredths

You'll need
★ Decimal & Fraction Relationships, pages 1 and 2 (Bridges Student Book, pages 141 and 142)

★ Home Connection 46, pages 133–136

★ overhead base ten pieces

★ class set of base ten pieces

★ half-class set of money value pieces

★ blank transparency

★ overhead pens

Exploring the Relationship Between Tenths and Fifths
Open today's session by asking students to organize their base ten pieces for easy use. Write $2/5$ on the overhead and ask students to discuss with their partners and neighbors how they could model the fraction with base ten pieces. Remind them to use the mat to represent a magnified unit and the smaller pieces to represent the fractional parts.

After students have had time to share their thinking in small groups, reconvene the class and have volunteers share how they would represent $2/5$ using base ten pieces. Ask them to show their models by arranging and labeling the overhead base ten pieces. Help support the connections students are making between fractions and decimals by recording their thoughts with equations on the whiteboard.

> ***Raina*** *At first we didn't think we could do it. Because the pieces are just ones, tenths, and hundredths. But then Larry said that if he put two striplets on the unit, it covered a fifth of the whole thing.*

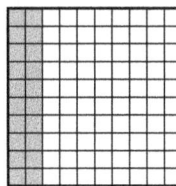

Teacher *So Raina and Larry, you said that two-tenths equal one-fifth. I'll write that in a couple of ways here on the board.*

$$\frac{1}{10} + \frac{1}{10} = \frac{1}{5}$$

$$2 \times \frac{1}{10} = \frac{1}{5}$$

$$\frac{2}{10} = \frac{1}{5}$$

Mark *I don't get that, Raina. How do you know it's a fifth? I can see it's two-tenths, but I don't see any fifths on there.*

Raina *Well, there are 10 tenths. So there are 5 groups of two-tenths. I'll mark them here. See?*

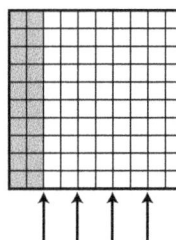

Mark *Oh, I see now. Thanks.*

Larry *So we doubled that. So four-tenths makes two-fifths.*

$$\frac{1}{10} + \frac{1}{10} + \frac{1}{10} + \frac{1}{10} = \frac{2}{5}$$

$$4 \times \frac{1}{10} = \frac{2}{5}$$

$$2 \times \frac{1}{5} = \frac{2}{5}$$

After students have clarified the relationship between tenths and fifths, ask them how $^2/_5$ could be recorded as a decimal number and record their suggestions beside the model on the overhead. Also invite them to share any other fractions that are equal to $^2/_5$ that they can see on the model, and record their suggestions beside the model as well.

Antoine *Well, it's 40 out of 100, so 40 over 100.*

Susie *I thought about it in tenths. It's four-tenths.*

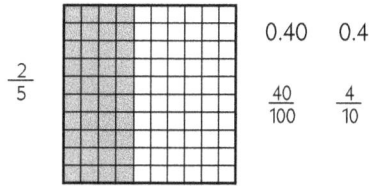

$\frac{2}{5}$ 0.40   0.4

$\frac{40}{100}$ $\frac{4}{10}$

Then ask students to build a model for $^3/_5$. Ask volunteers to recreate their model at the overhead, and then ask the class to come up with other fraction and decimal names for that amount based on what they can *see* in the model.

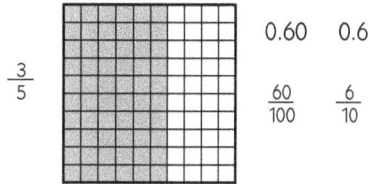

$\frac{3}{5}$ 0.60   0.6

$\frac{60}{100}$ $\frac{6}{10}$

Independent Investigations of Decimal and Fraction Relationships

After the class has discussed the models for $^2/_5$ and $^3/_5$, ask students to turn to Decimal & Fraction Relationships on pages 141 and 142 in their Bridges Student Books.

Bridges Student Book For use in Unit Six, Session 13.
NAME _____ DATE _____

Decimal & Fraction Relationships page 1 of 2

For each fraction below, use base ten pieces to find another fraction name and a decimal name that mean the same amount. Then sketch on the grid to prove you are correct. Be sure to label your sketches with numbers and/or words.

Fraction	Another Fraction Name	Decimal Name	Use the grid to show the fractions and decimals you named are equal.
example $\frac{1}{10}$	$\frac{10}{100}$	0.1	This is 10 hundredths and it also is 1 out of 10 columns.
1 $\frac{1}{2}$			
2 $\frac{1}{4}$			
3 $\frac{3}{4}$			

Bridges Student Book For use in Unit Six, Session 13.
NAME _____ DATE _____

Decimal & Fraction Relationships page 2 of 2

Fraction	Another Fraction Name	Decimal Name	Use the grid to show the fractions and decimals you named are equal.
4 $\frac{1}{20}$			
5 $\frac{1}{5}$			

CHALLENGE

Hint: If you divide the 10-by-10 grid into 8 equal parts, how many hundredths are in each part?

6 $\frac{1}{8}$			

Let students know that they can work alone or in pairs but that either way, they will each need to fill out their own pages. As they work, circulate around the room. If you notice that a particular fraction is causing confusion for many students, be sure to have the class discuss that fraction, either by having them pause during the work period to discuss it as a class or by reconvening the class at the end of the work period.

The last item is a challenge problem in which students are asked to represent $1/8$ as a decimal (0.125). Some students may consider the next stage of divisions and express the decimal to the thousandths place, while others may simply conclude correctly that $1/8$ is equal to a decimal somewhere between 0.12 and 0.13. Others, however, may report that $1/8$ is equivalent to twelve-and-a-half-hundredths. Most fourth graders haven't yet been introduced to thousandths, which will be explored in depth in fifth grade, so don't be alarmed if many students are unable to answer the challenge question correctly or do not attempt it.

HOME CONNECTION 46

At the end of the session, introduce Home Connection 46, which gives students another opportunity to see, sketch, and record equivalent fractions and decimals.

Decimal & Fraction Relationships page 1 of 2

For each fraction below, use base ten pieces to find another fraction name and a decimal name that mean the same amount. Then sketch on the grid to prove you are correct. Be sure to label your sketches with numbers and/or words.

Fraction	Another Fraction Name	Decimal Name	Use the grid to show the fractions and decimals you named are equal.
example $\frac{1}{10}$	$\frac{10}{100}$	0.1	This is 10 hundredths and it also is 1 out of 10 columns.
1 $\frac{1}{2}$			
2 $\frac{1}{4}$			
3 $\frac{3}{4}$			

Decimal & Fraction Relationships page 2 of 2

Fraction	Another Fraction Name	Decimal Name	Use the grid to show the fractions and decimals you named are equal.
4 $\frac{1}{20}$			
5 $\frac{1}{5}$			

CHALLENGE

Hint: If you divide the 10-by-10 grid into 8 equal parts, how many hundredths are in each part?

6 $\frac{1}{8}$			

Home Connection 46 ★ Worksheet

Decimals Are Fractions

1 This large square represents 1 unit.

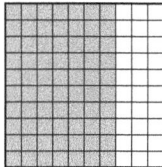

a How many tenths are shaded?

b How many hundredths are shaded?

2 Write the fraction name and the decimal name for each of the collections below. The first two are done as examples. As in the picture above, the large square represents 1 unit. The strip represents 1 tenth, and the smallest square represents 1 hundredth.

Collection	Fraction	Decimal
	$1\frac{2}{10}$	1.2
	$1\frac{15}{100}$	1.15
a		
b		

Collection	Fraction	Decimal
c		
d		
e		
f		

(Continued on back.)

© The Math Learning Center

111

3 Now draw a quick sketch of each of the fractions below and write its decimal name. The first two are done as examples.

Fraction	Sketch	Decimal
example $2\frac{3}{10}$		2.3
example $3\frac{6}{100}$		3.06
a $1\frac{9}{10}$		
b $3\frac{8}{10}$		
c $3\frac{3}{100}$		

(Continued on next page.)

Home Connection 46 Worksheet (cont.)

Fraction	Sketch	Decimal
d $2\frac{7}{10}$		
e $1\frac{2}{10}$		
f $1\frac{20}{100}$		
g $2\frac{5}{10}$		
h $2\frac{50}{100}$		

Source: From *Bridges in Mathematics: Grade 4, Teachers Guide* (Vol. 3, pp. 712–715), by R. Deerwater, A. E. Fischer, and A. Fisher, 2007, Salem, OR: The Math Learning Center. Copyright by The Math Learning Center. Reprinted with permission.

Lesson 13: Connecting Fractions and Decimals

Desired Outcomes

- Students will compare whole numbers, fractions, and decimals.
- Students will represent fractions and decimals in a variety of ways.
- Students will translate between fractions and decimals.

Teacher Information

In Lessons 13-16, students investigate the connections between and among fractions, decimals, and percents. Fractional numbers are compared, ordered, and applied to problem solving.

In Lesson 13, a number line provides a concrete model for comparing and ordering fractions and decimals. Number, area, and set representations of fractional numbers are compared and written in number sentences.

Teacher Preparation

- On a sheet of newsprint, prepare a chart with the title "Comparing Fractional Numbers."
- Display the Fraction Number Line in an area where students are able to attach cards.
- Have available the paper clips that have been prepared for the line. Display 0 and 1 placed 10 units apart on the number line.
- Prepare a well-mixed set of 20 or more cards from the Fraction Number Line Set for each group of four students. The cards should include all yellow number, area, and set cards; green decimal cards (except for percents); and blue whole number cards. The sets of cards will be used again in Lesson 14.
- Assemble for distribution: yellow fraction cards, green decimal cards, blue whole number cards, Student Record Books, and Bright Idea Pens.

Materials

For the class

1 sheet of newsprint
Fraction Number Line Set™
    Fraction Number Line
    Jumbo paper clips
    Blue whole number cards 0 to 1
1 black marker w/eraser
1 Bright Idea Marker w/Eraser

For each group of four students

20 or more decimal and fraction cards

For each student

Student Record Book
Bright Idea Pen

Vocabulary

Analyze: To examine the parts.

Decimal: A fractional number written in the base-10 place-value system containing a decimal point.

Decimal point: A dot written in a decimal number to indicate the place where values change from whole to fractional parts of 10.

Denominator: The bottom number in a fraction, which names the number of equal parts in the whole.

Equation: A mathematical statement that two things are equal, written with an equal sign.

Fraction: A number that names part of a whole unit or set, compares two amounts, or represents division.

Inequality: A mathematical statement which is not written with an equal sign.

Number sentence: A mathematical statement containing three parts: a left-side expression, a relation symbol, and a right-side expression.

Numerator: The top number in a fraction, which indicates the number of fractional units being counted.

Relationship: A meaningful connection.

Represent: To show in another way.

Procedure for the Lesson

Engage

Discussing Fractional Numbers

1. Explain that this lesson connects fractions and decimals, two types of fractional numbers. Mixed sets of fractions and decimals will be compared and ordered. Ask,

   What do you know about comparing fractions and decimals?

   What do you know about putting fractions and decimals in order?

2. Explain that sometimes people choose to use fractions to represent parts of wholes, and others choose decimals. Ask,

   What are examples of fractions used to represent parts of wholes in everyday life?

   What are examples of decimals used to represent parts of wholes in everyday life?

Investigate

Comparing Fractional Numbers

1. Arrange the students to work in groups of four, and distribute 20 or more fraction, decimal, and whole number cards to each group. Instruct the students to spread out their cards with the number face up so that everyone in their group can observe the set of cards.

2. Direct the students to discuss in their groups any relationships they see among the numbers in their set. After the discussion, ask,

   What did your group notice about the numbers represented on the cards?

   What else can be said about the cards in the sets?

3. Direct the students to identify several pairs of cards that show equalities, and pairs that show inequalities, using the cards in their set.

4. After an adequate amount of time, have each group choose one equality and inequality to share with the group. They should be prepared to explain how they know the numbers are equal to, greater than, or less than each other.

5. Give each group an opportunity to describe an equality and inequality. As the groups explain their pair of numbers, ask,

How do you know that pair of numbers is equal?

How do you know that pair of numbers represents an inequality?

Is there anyone that has a question or comment for this group?

6. Have the students sort their sets of cards so that tenths and any number, area, or set card with a fraction equal to one of the tenths are in one set. The remaining cards may be set aside. Display the Fraction Number Line with 0 and 1 placed 10 units apart.

7. Have each group identify any cards that show tenths represented as fractions, and place them on the number line. Next, have the groups identify tenths represented as fractions. Area models should be displayed next. After decimals, fractions, and area models are displayed, ask,

What patterns and relationships can be observed in the three representations for tenths that are displayed on the number line?

8. Lead a discussion about equivalent fractions for tenths (e.g., ⅕ = ²⁄₁₀, ⅖ = ⁴⁄₁₀). As each tenth is named, have the groups show their equivalent fractions and explain how they know that they are equivalent. Ask,

What knowledge about fractions is helping you identify equal fractions?

9. Display the chart with the title "Comparing Fractional Numbers" and draw a number line showing 10 units between 0 and 1, and 1 and 2. List several pairs of fractional numbers on the chart such as 0.4 and ⅖, ¹⁄₁₀ and 0.6, and 1.4 and 1¾. Have the students discuss in their groups which symbol (=, >, <) is needed to make each true number sentence. After the students have discussed the number sentences, ask,

Which symbol will make each number sentence true? Explain your thinking.

10. As the students explain their ideas to support the comparisons, summarize the thinking on the chart. Ask,

Which way to compare fractional numbers should you choose?

Comparing Fractional Numbers

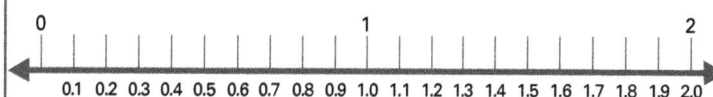

$0.4 = \frac{2}{5}$	$\frac{7}{10} > 0.6$	$1.4 < 1\frac{3}{4}$
We located 0.4 on the number line and counted fifths to verify that 0.4 and $\frac{2}{5}$ are equal. We thought of 0.4 as the fraction $\frac{4}{10}$ and simplified it to fifths.	We thought of the decimal 0.6 as a fraction and knew that seven-tenths is greater than six-tenths. We compared the two numbers on the number line and saw that $\frac{7}{10}$ was nearer 2 than 0.6.	We determined that $1\frac{3}{4}$ was between 1.7 and 1.8 on the number line by thinking about halves and fourths. We mentally changed 1.4 to $1\frac{16}{40}$, and $1\frac{3}{4}$ to $1\frac{30}{40}$. Since the whole numbers are the same, $\frac{16}{40} < \frac{30}{40}$.

11. Distribute the Student Record Books and Bright Idea Pens. Have the students locate the Reflective Practice for Lesson 13 in their Student Record Books. Instruct them to identify the symbol ($=$, $>$, $<$) that makes each number sentence true and explain their reasoning. Tell them that a number line is shown for each problem to help with comparisons.

12. As the students work, ask questions such as the following: *Are the different number lines providing ways to compare the numbers? How can the numbers be compared without the number lines?*

Reflect

Sharing Results

1. Choose several students to share their answers and explanations for the pairs of numbers on the Reflective Practice. Ask,

    Does anyone have a comment or question about the results or explanations?

2. Provide an opportunity for students to make changes in their work with the Bright Idea Pens.

Apply

Making Connections

The following activities can be used with whole groups, small groups, or individuals, depending on the needs of your students. The activities connect to past and future learning.

Literature Connections

Make available books that provide information about the connections between fractions, decimals, and percents, such as *Piece = Part = Portion: Fractions = Decimals = Percents* by Scott Gifford, *Delightful Decimals and Perfect Percents: Games and Activities That Make Math Easy and Fun* by Lynette Long, *Twizzlers Percentages Book* by Jerry Pallotta, or books that provide an everyday connection such as *The Report Card* by Andrew Clements and *The Everything Kids' Baseball Book: Today's Superstars, Great Teams, Legends—and Tips on Playing Like a Pro!* by Greg Jacobs.

Comparing Fractional Numbers

Arrange the students to work in groups of four. Distribute part of the cards from the Fraction Number Line Card Set to each group. Have the students each draw a pair of cards from their sets and explain to their group the relationship between their pair of numbers. Have each student draw a second pair of numbers and write a description of how to compare the numbers on notebook paper or other available paper.

Assessment

- Are students able to compare whole numbers, fractions, and decimals?
- Are students able to represent fractions and decimals in a variety of ways?
- Are students able to translate between fractions and decimals?

Information can be gathered from

Class Discussion

Teacher Observation

Individual and Group Questioning

Discussing Fractional Numbers

Comparing Fractional Numbers

Sharing Results

Student Record Book

Making Connections

Teacher Reflection

What did I learn about my students as they compared whole numbers, fractions, and decimals?

What did my students learn as they shared strategies for comparing fractional numbers?

Lesson 13: Connecting Fractions and Decimals
Reflective Practice

Name: _____   **Date:** _____

1. Write a symbol for greater than (>), less than (<), or equal to (=) to complete each number sentence.

```
      6                           7                           8
   ◄──┼─┼─┼─┼─┼─┼─┼─┼─┼─┼─┼─┼─┼─┼─┼─┼─┼─┼─┼─┼──►
      6.1 6.2 6.3 6.4 6.5 6.6 6.7 6.8 6.9 7.0 7.1 7.2 7.3 7.4 7.5 7.6 7.7 7.8 7.9 8.0
```

6.7 ____>____ $6\frac{1}{4}$	$\frac{72}{10}$ ____<____ 7.6
Write a description of your comparison strategy.	**Write a description of your comparison strategy.**
Descriptions will vary.	Descriptions will vary.

2. Describe a way to compare $6\frac{3}{5}$ with 6.4.

   Descriptions will vary.

Source: Clemson University, & Carolina Biological Supply Company. (2009). *Developing number concepts: Values and variables* (Math Out of the Box: Grade 5). Burlington, NC: Carolina Biological Supply Company. Reprinted with permission.

Handout 7.3C
Investigating Instructional Materials: Fourth Grade Lesson

Examine the lesson on Handout 7.3A and answer the questions below.

Lesson: *Bridges in Mathematics: Grade 4* (Vol. 3, pp. 712–715)

What big ideas, strategies, and mathematical models are being developed in this lesson?
What are the important mathematical concepts underlying the lesson? How does the lesson reflect the concepts from the Common Core State Standards?
What skills and knowledge are required for students to complete the tasks?

What are the benefits of using base-ten blocks to represent the value of fractions and decimals? What does the model help students see or understand about the relationship between fractions and decimals?

This lesson includes a sample class discussion. How does the teacher facilitate a discussion on the relationship between equivalent fractions and decimals? How does the teacher make connections between the model (base-ten blocks) and symbolic representations (equations)?

What are the strengths of this lesson?	What are some limitations, questions, and concerns that you have about the lesson?
	What misunderstandings and difficulties might your students encounter?

Handout 7.3D
Investigating Instructional Materials: Fifth Grade Lesson

Examine the lesson on Handout 7.3B and answer the questions below.

Lesson: *Math Out of the Box: Grade 5* (pp. 117–122)

What big ideas, strategies, and mathematical models are being developed in this lesson?
What are the important mathematical concepts underlying the lesson? How does the lesson reflect the concepts from the Common Core State Standards?
What skills and knowledge are required for students to complete the tasks?

What are the benefits of using the number line to represent the value of fractions and decimals? What does the model help students see or understand about the relationship between fractions and decimals?

The lesson asks students to identify pairs of number cards that show equalities and inequalities, followed by an explanation of why they think the pairs are either equal or unequal. How might your students justify whether or not pairs of number cards are either equal or unequal? What types of reasoning might they use?

What are the strengths of this lesson?	What are some limitations, questions, and concerns that you have about the lesson?
	What misunderstandings and difficulties might your students encounter?

Handout 7.3E
Investigating Your Instructional Materials: Analyzing Lessons

Examine a lesson from your instructional materials that focuses on connecting fractions and decimals and answer the questions below. You will use your responses to develop the lesson in Session 12.

Lesson: Pages:

What big ideas, strategies, and mathematical models are being developed in this lesson?
What are the important mathematical concepts underlying the lesson? How does the lesson reflect the concepts from the Common Core State Standards? What skills and knowledge are required for students to complete the tasks?
What are the similarities and differences between this lesson and the sample lesson from Handout 7.3A or 7.3B?

What are the strengths of this lesson?	What are some limitations, questions, and concerns that you have about the lesson?
	What misunderstandings and difficulties might your students encounter?

Handout 7.4

Student Connections: Fraction and Decimal Games

Select at least one of the games from Activity 7.2 to play with one small group of children. Write detailed notes below describing the strategies each student uses while solving a problem during the game.

Student 1	
Describe game situation and strategy.	
Student 2	
Describe game situation and strategy.	
Student 3	
Describe game situation and strategy.	

Session 8

Mathematical Models: Adding and Subtracting Fractions

Overview

How do models and understanding mathematical relationships help students develop fluency with addition and subtraction of fractions?

Description

Fluency with addition and subtraction of fractions does not depend solely on memorizing algorithms. Mathematical models can help students understand important relationships in the concepts for addition and subtraction of fractions.

Key Ideas

- Two essential foundations for understanding addition and subtraction of fractions with unlike denominators are (1) knowledge of strategies used to find equivalent fractions with like denominators and (2) comprehending that equivalent fractions have a constant ratio between the numerator and denominator.

- The ability to translate concepts among different representations is an important component of students' mathematical development.

- In order to use a model as a tool, the representation must make sense to the student.

Outline of Activities

- 8.1 Analyzing Student Connections: Mathematics Games   (15 minutes)
- 8.2 Models   (20 minutes)
- 8.3 Mathematical Models: Clocks and Number Lines   (30 minutes)
- 8.4 Adding Fractions: Why Doesn't $\frac{1}{2} + \frac{1}{3} = \frac{2}{5}$?   (15 minutes)
- 8.5 Before the Next Session   (5 minutes)
- 8.6 Lesson Design Notes   (5 minutes)

What to Bring

- Notes and student work: Student Connections activity (Handout 7.4)

To Complete Before Session 8

- Investigating Instructional Materials activity for lessons addressing addition and/or subtraction of decimals and/or fractions

Facilitator Notes   Session 8

Mathematical Models: Adding and Subtracting Fractions

If this is your first time facilitating the group, please refer to the more detailed facilitator guidelines in the Introduction. As the facilitator, it is generally your job to keep the conversation flowing and watch the clock. Use your judgment to decide when it's appropriate to extend a session for good conversation or when it's time to move on to the next activity. Remember to keep the group norms posted and revise them, as a group, as necessary.

Before the Session

- (There are no new handouts for Session 8.)
- Gather the following materials to be used in this session:
    - ☐ Group norms (from Activity 1.4)
- Remind team members to bring the following items from previous sessions:
    - ☐ Journal (and writing instruments)
    - ☐ Completed homework, Handout 7.4 Student Connections: Fraction and Decimal Games

During the Session

- Post group norms, and revise as a group as necessary.
- Activity 8.1: facilitate discussion and sharing.
- Activity 8.2: facilitate discussion.
- Activity 8.3: facilitate discussion.
- Activity 8.4: facilitate discussion.

After the Session

- Remind team members of homework, Identifying Instructional Materials activity for addition or subtraction of fractions or decimals.
- Pass any team materials on to the next facilitator.

Activity 8.1 Analyzing Student Connections: Mathematics Games

15 minutes   Handout 7.4 Student Connections: Fraction and Decimal Games

Your task from Session 7.4 was to select one of the games from Activity 7.2 to play with a small group of students and to record your observations on Handout 7.4.

Read your completed Student Connections activity, Handout 7.4, and the notes you wrote in your journal.

Share with your group the approaches your students used.

Discuss the following questions:

- Which game did you select and why?
- What strategies did children use to play each game? Was there anything that surprised you?
- What evidence was there that the game supported children in developing a conceptual understanding of comparing and ordering decimals and fractions?
- After watching your students play the game, how would you change or adapt the game to provide challenges at an appropriate level to meet the needs of all of your students?

Write in your journal about new insights you gained about your students during this activity. What new questions do you have about developing conceptual understanding and skill in comparing and ordering decimals and fractions? What new tasks or questions might help you to find out more about their thinking? What instructional strategies might help the struggling students you observed?

Activity 8.2 Models

20 minutes

A model is any object, picture, or drawing that represents a concept or on which the relationship for that concept can be imposed. Models are an essential part of learning and doing mathematics at all levels. "In a sense, models are mental maps mathematicians use as they organize their activity, solve problems, or explore relationships" (Fosnot & Dolk, 2002, p. 73). Because the number line is a model that provides a visual representation of the magnitude of and relationships between numbers, it can be a useful model for developing decimal concepts. There are other models for decimals that are also common in curriculum materials. You may be familiar with base-ten blocks, meter sticks, ten-by-ten grids, money, and other objects and diagrams used as models for decimal concepts.

Discuss the following questions:

- What models have you used when teaching decimal concepts? Share how you use these models.

- Which ones seem to be most helpful for students to develop understanding of decimal numbers? Why?

- Which ones are problematic because they are confusing or tend to limit students' decimal concepts? Why?

Read this excerpt from Van de Walle (2004), *Elementary and Middle School Mathematics: Teaching Developmentally:*

To "see" in a model the concept that it represents, you must already have that concept – that relationship – in your mind. If you did not, then you would have no relationship to impose on the model. This is precisely why models are often more meaningful to the teacher than to students. The teacher already has the concept and can see it in the model. A student without the concept sees only the physical object. Mathematical concepts that children are in the process of constructing are not the well-informed ideas conceived by adults. New ideas are formulated little by little over time. As children actively reflect on their new ideas, they test them out through as many different avenues as we might provide.... Models give learners something to think about, explore with, talk about, and reason with.

Three related uses for [models] in a developmental approach to teaching:
1. To help children develop new concepts or relationships.
2. To help children make connections between concepts and symbols.
3. To assess children's understanding. (p. 30)

Discuss the following questions:

- How do you react to the statement in the excerpt, "This is precisely why models are often more meaningful to the teacher than to students"? Have you found it to be true that students sometimes do not see the mathematics in a model?

- Van de Walle suggests that models can help teachers assess children's understanding. Have you experienced this? How?

Activity 8.3 Mathematical Models: Clocks and Number Lines

30 minutes

Students can use the clock as a model to help them understand how to add and subtract fractions with unlike denominators. In the following vignette, Ms. Nape's class has used the clock as a model for finding fractional equivalents and will now use it to add fractions with unlike denominators. Ms. Nape poses this problem:

$$\frac{1}{3} + \frac{1}{4}$$

Solve this problem using a clock as a model. First work individually and then, after several minutes, share your approach with others in your group. Discuss how your strategies are similar to or different from one another.

Read the following vignette to see how Ms. Nape's students approached the problem and to identify questions she might ask next.

Ms. Nape: How could we use a clock to help us solve the following number sentence?

$$\frac{1}{3} + \frac{1}{4}$$

Patrick: Well, a third of an hour is 20 minutes and a fourth of an hour is 15 minutes, so one-third [⅓] plus one-fourth [¼] of an hour is 35 minutes. But I don't think one-third [⅓] plus one-fourth [¼] is 35. That doesn't make any sense at all. And one-third [⅓] and one-fourth [¼] are both smaller than one. How can the answer be 35?

Julio: What Patrick said is right, but he forgot that we are looking at parts of an *hour*, and 35 minutes is thirty-five–sixtieths [$^{35}\!/_{60}$] of an hour. I think the answer is thirty-five-sixtieths [$^{35}\!/_{60}$], but I'm not sure if I can prove it.

Tanya: I was thinking about it a different way. I know that one-third [⅓] of an hour is 20 minutes and that means the big hand would be pointing to the 4 on the clock. The clock is divided into 12 parts if you look at the numbers on the clock, so I think one-third [⅓] shows four-twelfths [$^{4}\!/_{12}$] of the hour, right? One-fourth of an hour is 15 minutes and the big hand points to the 3. That means that one-fourth [¼] is three-twelfths [$^{3}\!/_{12}$]. If you put three-twelfths [$^{3}\!/_{12}$] together with four-twelfths [$^{4}\!/_{12}$] you get seven-twelfths [$^{7}\!/_{12}$]. But that's not what Julio got. Who's right?

Discuss the following questions:

- What do Patrick, Julio, and Tanya understand about adding fractions with unlike denominators? What are their areas of confusion?
- How do you think Ms. Nape should proceed? What questions should she ask? What diagrams or models could she suggest?
- How do you think the students would have solved an addition problem with related fractions such as ⅜ + ¼, using the clock as a model?
- How would students solve a subtraction problem, such as ⅓ − ¼, using the clock as a model?

Another model Ms. Nape's students have used is parallel number lines showing equal parts.

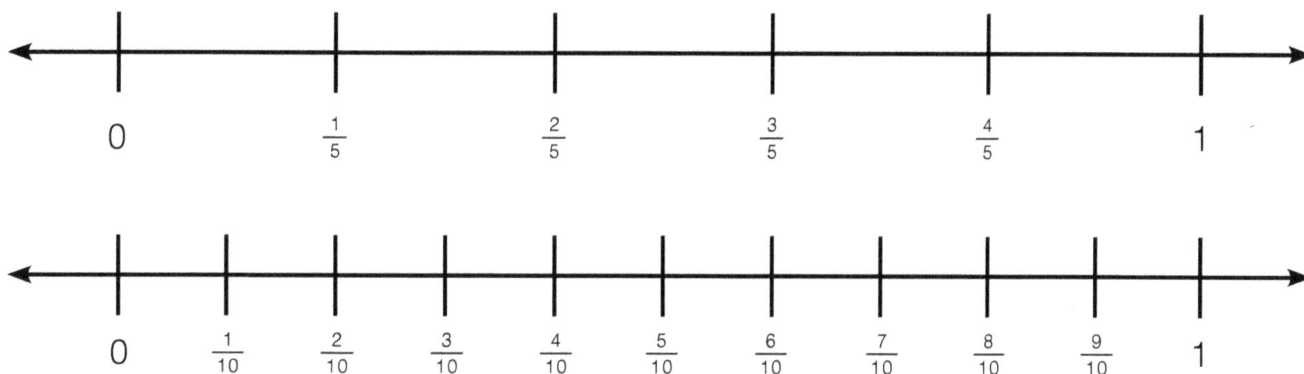

On a different day, Ms. Nape posed the following problem:

$$\frac{2}{5} + \frac{1}{10}$$

Read the following vignette to see how Ms. Nape's students approached the problem and identify questions she might ask next.

Ms. Nape: How could we use parallel number lines to help us add two-fifths [$\frac{2}{5}$] plus one-tenth [$\frac{1}{10}$]?

Paul: I don't need a number line. I can just add 2 plus 1 to get 3 on top. And add 5 plus 10 to get 15 on the bottom. The answer is three-fifteenths [$\frac{3}{15}$]. It's easy!

Lisa: I don't think that can be right. I mean, two-fifths [$\frac{2}{5}$] is almost half and you are adding some more. And three-fifteenths [$\frac{3}{15}$] is *way* less than half. Something isn't right here.

Claire: Wait a minute. Look at the number lines! If you line up the fifths number line and the tenths number line you can see that two-fifths [$\frac{2}{5}$] and four-tenths [$\frac{4}{10}$] line up. If you add another one-tenth [$\frac{1}{10}$] to four-tenths [$\frac{4}{10}$] you would get five-tenths [$\frac{5}{10}$].

Lisa: That makes sense! Because five-tenths [$\frac{5}{10}$] is equal to one-half [$\frac{1}{2}$] and that's like what I predicted.

Paul: I get what Lisa and Claire just said, but I don't see why my way doesn't work. It seems so logical.

Discuss how you think Ms. Nape should proceed. What questions should she ask? What diagrams or models could she suggest?

Discuss the following questions:

- What do Paul, Lisa, and Claire understand about adding related fractions? What are their areas of confusion?

- How do you think Ms. Nape should proceed? What questions should she ask? What diagrams or models could she suggest?

- How do you think the students would have solved an addition problem with like and unlike denominators such as $\frac{2}{5} + \frac{1}{2}$, using parallel number lines as a model?

- How would students solve a subtraction problem with unlike denominators, such as $\frac{2}{3} - \frac{1}{4}$, using parallel number lines as a model?

Discuss the following questions with your group:

- How does Ms. Nape structure these lessons to help students develop proficiency in adding and subtracting fractions with related and unlike denominators?

- Have you used the clock or parallel number lines as models for adding and subtracting fractions? Do you think they would be effective models for your students? Why or why not?

- In Session 4, you explored the use of square tiles as a model. How does this model compare with clocks and number lines?

- Which of these models would you like to add to your components of a learning landscape (Handout 2.3 in your journal)?

Activity 8.4 Adding Fractions: Why Doesn't $\frac{1}{2} + \frac{1}{3} = \frac{2}{5}$?

---

15 minutes

Recall in Activity 8.3 that Paul tried to solve $\frac{2}{5} + \frac{1}{10}$ by adding the numerators and the denominators. His initial solution to the problem was $\frac{3}{15}$. This is one of the most common errors students make when adding fractions. It results when they apply whole-number concepts separately to the numerators and then the denominators of the fractions being added. This illustrates a misconception that the numerals that make up a fraction represent two separate numbers rather than one quantity.

Discuss the following questions:

- Have you seen this error in the work of your students? How have you tried to help them understand and correct this error?

- What are some big ideas that support understanding of addition of fractions with related or unlike denominators? Which of these big ideas can you add to the learning landscape?

- How might the use of various models help students understand and correct this misconception?

Activity 8.5 Before the Next Session

5 minutes

Instructional Materials for Addition or Subtraction of Fractions or Decimals

In Session 9, you will analyze lessons that address addition and subtraction of fractions and decimals. Between now and the next session, identify a lesson on these topics from your instructional materials. You might select a lesson that you have not taught before, one that you particularly enjoy teaching, or one that is challenging to teach.

The activity in Session 9 will focus on these questions:

- What big ideas, strategies, and mathematical models are being developed in the lesson?
- What skills and knowledge are required to complete the tasks?
- What are the important mathematical concepts underlying the lesson?
- What are the strengths of the lesson?
- What are some limitations, questions, and concerns that you have about the lesson?

Activity 8.6 Lesson Design Notes

5 minutes

The key ideas for this session are

- Two essential foundations for understanding addition and subtraction of fractions with unlike denominators are (1) knowledge of strategies used to find equivalent fractions with like denominators, and (2) comprehending that equivalent fractions have a constant ratio between the numerator and denominator.
- The ability to translate concepts among different representations is an important component of students' mathematical development.
- In order to use a model as a tool, the representation must make sense to the student.

Reflect on what you learned during this session and how the ideas apply to each of the three themes in your Lesson Design Notes. A few prompts related to the themes follow. These are merely suggestions and should not limit your reflection or the ideas you capture.

- Where do you want to go?
  - In Activity 8.3, you examined addition of fractions with unlike denominators. What big ideas do you want your students to understand in order to become proficient with these types of problems?

- Where are you now?
  - In Activity 8.1, you discussed the strategies students used to play games that focus on comparing and ordering fractions and decimals. What did you learn that helps you identify where your students are in their understanding of rational numbers?
- What is the best way to get there?
  - In Activity 8.3, you explored clocks and number lines. How can these models be used to support students in building their proficiency with addition and subtraction with fractions?

References and Resources

Barnett, C., Goldenstein, D., & Jackson, B. (Eds.). (1994). *Fractions, decimals, ratios, and percents: Hard to teach and hard to learn?* Portsmouth, NH: Heinemann.

Fosnot, C. T., & Dolk, M. (2002). *Young mathematicians at work: Constructing fractions, decimals and percents.* Portsmouth, NH: Heinemann.

Van de Walle, J. A. (2004). *Elementary and middle school mathematics: Teaching developmentally* (4th ed.). New York: Longman.

Session 9

Mathematical Games: Adding and Subtracting Fractions and Decimals

How can mathematical games help students develop fluency with addition and subtraction of fractions and decimals?

Description

Mathematical games can promote learning and enhance students' ability to solve problems involving addition and subtraction of fractions and decimals. Teachers can use games to help build students' fluency with adding and subtracting fractions and decimals.

Key Ideas

- Mathematical games can provide an engaging context for students to learn and practice addition and subtraction with fractions and decimals.

- Common student errors in addition and subtraction of decimals may stem from inappropriate application of whole-number rules and relationships to decimals.

- It is important to look critically at instructional materials and identify how they support students' understanding of fractions and decimals.

Outline of Activities

- 9.1 Investigating Instructional Materials: (20 minutes)
  Adding and Subtracting Fractions and Decimals

- 9.2 Mathematical Games: Adding and   (45 minutes)
  Subtracting Fractions and Decimals

- 9.3 Identifying and Correcting Common Decimal Errors   (15 minutes)

- 9.4 Before the Next Session   (5 minutes)

- 9.5 Lesson Design Notes   (5 minutes)

What to Bring

- Handouts 4.4 and 6.3 from previous sessions

- Instructional materials: lessons addressing addition and/or subtraction of decimals and/or fractions

- Common Core State Standards: Standards for Mathematical Content

To Complete Before Session 10

- Student Connections: Observing Children Playing Games (Handout 9.4)

Facilitator Notes   Session 9

Mathematical Games: Adding and Subtracting Fractions and Decimals

If this is your first time facilitating the group, please refer to the more detailed facilitator guidelines in the Introduction. As the facilitator, it is generally your job to keep the conversation flowing and watch the clock. Use your judgment to decide when it's appropriate to extend a session for good conversation or when it's time to move on to the next activity. Remember to keep the group norms posted and revise them, as a group, as necessary.

Before the Session

- Make copies of the following handouts for each team member:
    - ☐ 9.1A: Sample Lesson: Fourth Grade
    - ☐ 9.1B Sample Lesson: Fifth Grade
    - ☐ 9.1C: Investigating Instructional Materials: Fourth Grade Lesson
    - ☐ 9.1D: Investigating Instructional Materials: Fifth Grade Lesson
    - ☐ 9.1E: Investigating Your Instructional Materials: Analyzing Lessons
    - ☐ 9.2A: Mathematics Games: Adding and Subtracting Fractions and Decimals
    - ☐ 9.2B: Beat the Clock Recording Sheet
    - ☐ 9.2C: Beat the Clock Fraction Cards
    - ☐ 9.2D: Estimating Sums Game Cards
    - ☐ 9.2E: Estimating Sums Fraction Cards
    - ☐ 9.2F: One Hundredth to One Chart
    - ☐ 9.2G: Take Five Decimal Cards
    - ☐ 9.2H: Close to Two Grids
    - ☐ 9.2I: Close to Two Spinners
    - ☐ 9.2J: High Five Cards
    - ☐ 9.2K: High Five Recording Sheet
    - ☐ 9.4: Student Connections: Observing Children Playing Games

- Gather the following materials to be used in this session:
    - ☐ Group norms (from Activity 1.4)
    - ☐ Prepared sets of game cards (Handouts 9.2C, 9.2D, 9.2E, 9.2G, and 9.2J) on two colors of card stock (see Handout 9.2A)
    - ☐ Scissors
    - ☐ Game pieces
    - ☐ Transparent counters or chips
    - ☐ Paper clips

- Remind team members to bring the following items from previous sessions:
  - ☐ Journal (and writing instruments)
  - ☐ Completed homework, Identifying Instructional Materials activity addressing addition and/or subtraction of decimals and/or fractions
  - ☐ Handout 4.4 Common Core State Standards and Handout 6.3 Five Strands of Mathematical Proficiency
  - ☐ Common Core State Standards: Standards for Mathematical Content

During the Session

- Post group norms, and revise as a group as necessary.
- Activity 9.1: facilitate discussion; facilitate partnering, if necessary.
- Activity 9.2: facilitate discussion and sharing; facilitate partnering, if necessary.
- Activity 9.3: facilitate discussion; facilitate partnering, if necessary.

After the Session

- Remind team members of homework, Handout 9.4 Student Connections: Observing Children Playing Games.
- Pass any team materials to the next facilitator.

Activity 9.1 Investigating Instructional Materials: Adding and Subtracting Fractions and Decimals

20 minutes

Handout 4.4 Common Core State Standards
Handout 6.3 Five Strands of Mathematical Proficiency
Handout 9.1A Sample Lesson: Fourth Grade
Handout 9.1B Sample Lesson: Fifth Grade
Handout 9.1C Investigating Instructional Materials: Fourth Grade Lesson
Handout 9.1D Investigating Instructional Materials: Fifth Grade Lesson
Handout 9.1E Investigating Your Instructional Materials: Analyzing Lessons
Instructional Materials: Lessons on adding/subtracting fractions/decimals
Common Core State Standards: Standards for Mathematical Content

Review the sample lesson for your grade level Handout 9.1A or 9.1B with a partner.

Try some of the lesson activities. Look closely at the lesson and consider the questions that follow. Handouts 9.1C and 9.1D list the same questions in a table where you can record your responses.

- What big ideas, strategies, and mathematical models are being developed in the lesson? (See Handout 2.3 in your journal.)

- What are the important mathematical concepts underlying the lesson? How does the lesson reflect the concepts from the Common Core State Standards? (See Handout 4.4 and Standards for Mathematical Content for your grade level.)

- What skills and knowledge are required to complete the tasks?

- Which strands of mathematical proficiency (see Handout 6.3) are represented in this lesson?

- For the fourth grade lesson, discuss the following questions:
  o On pages 147 and 148, the lesson has students adding decimals from left to right and then from right to left. How are these two approaches different? What are the benefits of each approach? How does each approach help students develop procedural fluency?

- For the fifth grade lesson, discuss the following questions:
  o How is the lesson designed to help students make sense of adding and subtracting fractions with unlike denominators? What types of questions does the teacher ask students? Which models help illustrate the meanings of the problems?

- What are the strengths of the lesson?

- What are some limitations, questions, and concerns that you have about the lesson? What misunderstandings and difficulties might your students encounter?

Repeat the process above with a lesson from your own curriculum. In your homework from Session 8, you may have selected a lesson for analysis that focuses on the same topic or concepts as the sample lesson. You can analyze the same lesson as a group or work individually on different lessons. Handout 9.1E includes a table similar to the one from Handouts 9.1C and 9.1D and should be used to record your observations about the lesson from your curriculum.

Discuss responses on both handouts as a group. What portions of these lessons might you combine to make the learning experience stronger for your students?

Activity 9.2 Mathematical Games: Adding and Subtracting Fractions and Decimals

45 minutes   Handout 9.2A Mathematics Games: Adding and Subtracting Fractions and Decimals
Handout 9.2B Beat the Clock Recording Sheet
Handout 9.2C Beat the Clock Fraction Cards
Handout 9.2D Estimating Sums Game Cards
Handout 9.2E Estimating Sums Fraction Cards
Handout 9.2F One Hundredth to One Chart
Handout 9.2G Take Five Decimal Cards
Handout 9.2H Close to Two Grids
Handout 9.2I Close to Two Spinners
Handout 9.2J High Five Cards
Handout 9.2K High Five Recording Sheet
Game pieces, transparent counters or chips, paper clips, and scissors

As you discussed in Session 7, games can provide motivating opportunities for students to practice addition and subtraction of rational numbers. Most students need to use mathematics concepts in many different contexts before becoming truly proficient with them. Consider the benefits of providing practice using games that engage students at a higher level of cognitive demand. Games can also help students become more independent when they are structured so that the players decide when an answer is correct, rather than relying on the teacher to validate answers. Each of the games in this activity engages students in a context for practicing adding and subtracting fractions and/or decimals.

Read the descriptions of the five games on Handout 9.2A.

Play each game with a partner.

Discuss each game with your partner using the following questions:

- What logic or strategy did you use while playing this game? How might this game help students develop a conceptual understanding of the addition and subtraction of decimals and/or fractions? How might each game promote mental computation skill?

- What variations to the rules or structure could be made that would make the game more or less challenging for some of your students? How might the games be changed to focus on subtraction with fractions or decimals?

- What strategies would students use to play each game? What would you look for as you observe students? What questions would you ask students as they play or after the game is finished to assess their level of numerical reasoning?

Share your discussion with the group, using the following question:

- How does each game help students develop understanding of and fluency with the addition and subtraction of rational numbers?

Reflect and record ideas in your journal about how you could use games to help your students develop meaning of rational numbers, effective strategies for solving problems, and fluency in adding and subtracting fractions and decimals.

Activity 9.3 Identifying and Correcting Common Decimal Errors

15 minutes   Handout 6.3 Five Strands of Mathematical Proficiency

Gaining conceptual understanding for addition and subtraction with decimals and fractions is an important milestone in student learning. Often the error patterns in students' computation with decimals reveal gaps in their conceptual understanding. Teachers who detect and respond to these errors can provide learning activities that address these misunderstandings.

Review the definition of conceptual understanding on Handout 6.3.

Discuss with a partner specific examples that would indicate that a student has conceptual understanding of addition and subtraction with decimals and fractions. What instructional activities could support children in developing this kind of conceptual understanding?

Traditionally, when teaching addition and subtraction with decimals, instruction has emphasized the memorization of rules and procedures. Yet many children consistently make common errors when computing with decimal numbers.

Work with a partner and discuss some common errors students make when adding and subtracting decimals. Make a list that includes an example of each error. What misconceptions about decimals might lead to the errors you identified?

Examine these student errors:

Saul: $0.09 + 0.07 = 0.016$

Anna: $0.7 + 0.5 = 0.12$

Colby: $0.5 - 0.01 = .4$

Discuss the following questions:

- What error did students each make in their response?

- What logic might these students have used to get these answers? Which of these are similar to examples you identified in your list?

- What misconception does this reveal about the students' understanding of decimal numbers?

Read the following research quotation:

> Many of the errors that children make when working with decimals suggest that they are applying whole-number rules and procedures to decimal numbers. . . . In the United States, the whole-number-rule pattern is the most commonly occurring error pattern among children who are just beginning to work with decimals, and children are making sense of the decimal-fraction system by trying to connect it with the kind of number system of which they already have some working knowledge. (Schifter, Bastable, & Russell, 1999, pp. 145–177)

Discuss the following questions:

- In the examples, in what ways do the student errors illustrate misapplying whole-number rules and procedures to decimals? What do these errors indicate about their understanding of place value?

- Review the other common errors you wrote on your list. Do they illustrate misapplication of whole number rules and procedures? If not, what other misconceptions do you think contribute to these errors?

Activity 9.4 Before the Next Session

5 minutes   Handout 9.2A Mathematics Games: Adding and Subtracting Fractions and Decimals

Handout 9.4 Student Connections: Observing Children Playing Games

Cards, recording sheets, and spinners (see Handouts 9.2B–9.2K)

Before the next session, select one of the games from Activity 9.2 to play with a small group of students. Sit with the group as they play the game and record what each student says and does. Record your observations on Handout 9.4. Try to be as detailed as possible in describing how each student approaches the game, the strategies they use, what errors they make, and anything else of interest that happens during the observation.

Write in your journal about what you learned about student thinking while observing the students playing these games. What approaches did students use? Was there anything that surprised you? How will you use this information to design learning experiences for your students on addition and subtraction with fractions and decimals?

Activity 9.5 Lesson Design Notes

5 minutes

The key ideas for this session are

- Mathematical games can provide an engaging context for students to learn and practice addition and subtraction with fractions and decimals.
- Common student errors in addition and subtraction of decimals may stem from inappropriate application of whole-number rules and relationships to decimals.
- It is important to look critically at instructional materials and identify how they support students' understanding of fractions and decimals.

Reflect on what you learned during this session and how the ideas apply to each of the three themes in your Lesson Design Notes. A few prompts related to the themes follow. These are merely suggestions and should not limit your reflection or the ideas you capture.

- Where do you want to go?
  - In Activity 9.2, you played a number of games that focus on addition and subtraction with fractions and decimals. What logic or strategies would you like your students to use as they play these games?
- Where are you now?
  - In Activity 9.3, you examined common decimal errors. Which of your students exhibit these errors? What types of interventions could you try with students who exhibit these errors?
- What is the best way to get there?
  - In Activity 9.1, you analyzed sample lessons. What ideas from the sample lessons are you interested in trying out in your classroom?

References and Resources

Clemson University, & Carolina Biological Supply Company. (2009). *Developing number concepts: Stories and statements. Math out of the box: Grade 4.* Burlington, NC: Carolina Biological Supply Company.

Deerwater, R., Fischer, A. E., & Fisher, A. (2007). *Bridges in Mathematics: Grade 5, Teachers Guide* (Vol. 3). Salem, OR: The Math Learning Center.

Kilpatrick, J., Swafford, J., & Findell, B. (Eds.). (2001). *Adding it up: Helping children learn mathematics.* Washington, DC: National Academies Press.

Schifter, D., Bastable, V., Russell, S. J. (1999). *Building a system of tens: Casebook.* Parsippany, NJ: Dave Seymour.

Van de Walle, J. A. (2009). *Elementary and middle school mathematics: Teaching developmentally* (7th ed.). Needham Heights, MA: Allyn & Bacon.

Lesson 11: Adding Decimals

Desired Outcomes

- Students will investigate models for adding decimals.
- Students will analyze and apply strategies for adding decimals.
- Students will estimate sums of decimal numbers using rounding.

Teacher Information

In this lesson, students apply their knowledge of decimals to addition. They review strategies used in the past to regroup numbers connected to the base-10 place-value system.

Students share their strategies for addition and analyze the reasonableness of the sums of addition problems using rounding as an estimation strategy. This lesson builds skills that lead toward fluency in the operation of addition.

Teacher Preparation

- On the sheet of newsprint, prepare a chart with the title "Adding and Subtracting Decimals." This chart will be used again in Lesson 12.
- Prepare a mixed set of blue whole number cards and green decimal cards with at least 1 whole number, 1 tenth, and 1 hundredth card for each group of four students.
- Assemble for distribution: Student Record Books and Bright Idea Pens.
- Provide access to notebook paper, which is not provided in the kit.

Procedure for the Lesson

Engage

Discussing Decimals

1. Arrange the students to work in groups of four. Distribute a mixed set of decimal and whole number cards to each group so that each student has one card.

2. Have the students display the cards so that the students in their group can observe the cards. Direct the students in a group to compare the cards and tell their group what they notice. Ask,

   In what ways are the numbers on the cards similar? Different?

Materials

For the class

1 black marker w/eraser
Bright Idea Marker w/Eraser
1 sheet of newsprint
Bright Idea Marker w/Eraser

For each group of four students

4 cards from the set of Blue whole number cards 1–20 and Green decimal number cards 0.1–0.9 and 0.01–0.10

For each student

Student Record Book
Bright Idea Pen

Needed but not supplied

Notebook paper

Vocabulary

Addend: A number that is added to another number or numbers.

Analyze: To examine the parts.

Decimal: A fractional number written in the base-10 place-value system containing a decimal point.

Decimal point: A dot written in a decimal number to indicate the place where values change from whole to fractional parts of 10.

Estimate: An approximation based on known information.

Sum: The result of addition.

What can be said about place value and the numbers on the cards?

3. Have the students place a whole number and a tenth card side by side to make a mixed number. Call on several students to explain a way to round the number to the nearest whole number.

4. Have the students place a whole number and a hundredth card side by side to make a mixed number. Call on several students to explain a way to round the number to the nearest whole number. Explain that rounding will be used as an estimation strategy to judge the reasonableness of the answers in this lesson.

Investigate

Adding Decimals

1. Direct the students in each group to determine a sum for the numbers shown on their set of cards. After the students have determined the sums, ask,

   What process did you use to add the numbers?

   Did you add whole numbers or decimals first? Explain.

2. Explain that strategies used to add whole numbers can also be used to add decimal numbers. Choose a group to read the numbers on their cards. As they read the numbers, write them on the chart in a column with place values lined up vertically. Ask,

   What is the place value of each of the columns?

   How does the decimal point aid in knowing the place value of the numbers?

3. Explain that zeros can be filled in on the decimal side so that there is a digit for each number in each column. Add zeros to the numbers.

4. Collect the cards and write a number with digits having place values up to thousands and decimals in the tenths and hundredths, such as 347.5 + 268.45. Arrange the numbers in columns and label the columns with their place values.

5. Have a student add each place value aloud from left to right as the sums are recorded on the chart. Next, have one of the students mentally add the resulting sums (e.g., 500.00 + 100.00 + 15.00 + .90 + .05). Lead a discussion about this strategy of adding left to right. Ask,

   What experiences have you had with this strategy for adding large numbers?

   What is a description of the way this strategy works?

Adding and Subtracting Decimals

Adding the Sum of the Sums

H	T	O	T	H	
3	4	7	.5	0	
+ 2	6	8	.4	5	Add the hundreds.
5	0	0	.0	0	Add the tens.
1	0	0	.0	0	Add the ones.
	1	5	.0	0	Add the tenths.
			.9	0	Add the hundredths.
			.0	5	Determine the sum
6	1	5	.9	5	of the sums.

6. Use the same numbers to review another algorithm that adds from right to left. Set up the problem in the same way with the place values labeled. Explain that with this strategy each place value is added and adjusted by regrouping so that the numbers stay true to their place values.

7. Select a student to add each column in turn from right to left. As a sum is determined for a column, ask if there is an amount that needs to be regrouped. If there is a need to regroup, move the digit to the next place on the left until the sum is determined.

Adding and Subtracting Decimals

Adding With Regrouping

H	T	O	T	H
1	1			
3	4	7	.5	0
+ 2	6	8	.4	5
6	1	5	.9	5

The ones column required regrouping because 7 + 8 = 15. One ten was moved to the tens column. The tens column required regrouping because 40 + 60 + 10 = 110. One hundred was moved to the hundreds column.

Rounding to Estimate

$$\begin{array}{r} 300.00 \\ + 300.00 \\ \hline 600.00 \end{array}$$

The sums of 600 and 615.95 are fairly close, indicating that our answer is reasonable.

8. To check the reasonableness of an answer when working with large numbers, rounding to the left-most place value provides a strategy for estimation. Lead a discussion about using rounding to check the reasonableness of the answer. Show the rounding on the chart as the students explain it. Ask,

Which is the left-most place value used in this problem?

What are the addends when rounded to the hundreds place?

In what way does the rounding sum compare with the first sum to show the reasonableness of the answer?

9. Repeat the adding and rounding of a variety of decimal numbers as needed by the students. Next, distribute the Student Record Books and have the students locate the Reflective Practice for Lesson 11. Tell the students to use a strategy of their choice to solve the problems. Direct them to show the rounding estimate in the first set of problems. Encourage the students to mentally round the numbers as a way to efficiently check the reasonableness of their answers in the second set. Students may need access to notebook paper for some of their computation, depending on their strategy.

10. As the students work, ask questions such as the following:
What strategies are you using to determine the sums?
What place-value patterns do you notice as you are adding?
Are your estimates and sums about the same?

Reflect

Comparing Results

1. Have the students meet back in their groups. Provide access to the Bright Idea Pens. Direct the students to compare their answers on the Reflective Practice for Lesson 11.

2. Direct them to analyze the problems when sums are not the same. Explain that if any changes are made, they should be made with the Bright Idea Pens. After the groups have met, ask,

Did discussing the problems reveal any misunderstandings that need to be discussed with the whole group?

What changes, if any, did you make in your work?

3. Discuss using rounding as an estimation strategy. Ask,

In what way was the rounding strategy valuable in knowing whether your answer was reasonable?

Making Connections

The following activities can be used with whole groups, small groups, or individuals, depending on the needs of your students. The activities connect to past and future learning.

Adding Decimals

Make the whole number cards and decimal number cards available for practicing quick mental addition. Have each student working in a small group of students choose and display a whole number or decimal card. Direct the students to try to be the first to mentally determine the sum of the numbers. The students should verify the answer with paper and pencil or calculators.

Rounding Thousandths

Have the students work in pairs to write a strategy for rounding thousandths to the nearest hundredth. Provide a list of numbers, such as .701, 10.245, .428, and .021. Have the students share their strategies for rounding to the nearest hundredth.

Home Connection 11

Have the students take home Home Connection 11. Explain that the examples of decimals that are returned will be used in a classroom display. Plan to display the work in a place where students can analyze the ways that decimals are used in everyday life.

What did I learn about my students' prior experiences with addition?

What did my students learn as they shared strategies for adding decimals?

Assessment

- Are students able to investigate models for adding decimals?
- Are students able to analyze and apply strategies for adding decimals?
- Are students able to estimate sums of decimal numbers using rounding?

Information can be gathered from

Class Discussion
Teacher Observation
Individual and Group Questioning
Discussing Decimals
Adding Decimals
Comparing Results
Student Record Book
Making Connections

Lesson 11: Adding Decimals
Reflective Practice

Name: _____ **Date:** _____

1. Determine the sums using a strategy of your choice. Show your rounding estimate. Compare the two sums to determine the reasonableness of your answer.

Solve the problem.

```
T  H  T  O  T  H
   7  3  8 .1  7
+  1  4  2 .4  4
───────────────
   8  8  0 .6  1
```

Show rounding to the nearest hundred.

```
  700
+ 100
─────
  800
```

Solve the problem.

```
T  H  T  O  T  H
5, 6  1  6 .4  2
+ 1,5 5  3 .7  4
───────────────
7, 1  7  0 .1  6
```

Show rounding to the nearest hundred.

```
  5,600
+ 1,600
───────
  7,200
```

Solve the problem.

```
T  H  T  O  T  H
   7  9  8 .2  1
+     9  4 .5  8
───────────────
   8  9  2 .7  9
```

Show rounding to the nearest hundred.

```
  800
+ 100
─────
  900
```

2. **Determine the sums using a strategy of your choice. Mentally estimate with rounding. Compare the two sums to determine the reasonableness of your answer.**

758.2	.53	9,269.82	.9
+ 328.9	+ .64	+ 74.10	+ .9
1,087.1	1.17	9,343.92	1.8

510.3	.71	2,173.77	.41
+ 368.1	+ .99	+ 4,627.13	+ .09
878.4	1.70	6,800.90	.50

638	4,600.17	.4	63.9
+ 562	+ 4,600.93	+ .9	+ 27.2
1,200	9,201.10	1.3	91.1

3. **Explain the way you mentally used rounding to check the reasonableness of your answers. Explain any sums that were not near your estimates.**

Explanations will vary.

Source: Clemson University, & Carolina Biological Supply Company. (2009). *Developing number concepts: Stories and statements* (Math Out of the Box). Burlington, NC: Carolina Biological Supply Company. Reprinted with permission.

Handout 9.1B
Sample Lesson: Fifth Grade

Session 5

Adding & Subtracting Fractions, Part 1 of 2

Overview

Students discuss equivalent fractions on a clock face and then solve a series of story problems together that require them to make some generalizations based on their own experiences and observations about adding and subtracting fractions with like and unlike denominators.

Actions

1   Students discuss Home Connection 50, Equivalent Fractions on a Clock.

2   Students solve a series of fraction story problems together and develop some generalizations about adding and subtracting fractions.

Skills & Concepts

★ finding equivalent fractions

★ adding and subtracting fractions with like and unlike denominators

★ investigating common denominators

★ identifying common factors of a set of whole numbers

★ finding and describing patterns to help solve problems

★ solving problems involving elapsed time

You'll need

★ Equivalent Fractions on a Clock (Overhead 6.3)

★ Fractions of an Hour Story Problems (Overhead 6.4)

★ Home Connection 50, Equivalent Fractions on a Clock (completed by students after Session 4)

★ overhead pens

★ piece of paper to mask portions of the overhead

★ students' fraction kits

★ chart about generating equivalent fractions from Session 4

★ a piece of chart paper (optional)

STUDENT JOURNAL

Discussing Equivalent Fractions on a Clock

Ask students to get out the homework they completed last night, Equivalent Fractions on a Clock (Home Connection 50). Give them a few minutes to pair-share the fractions they found for each clock. Invite them to add more fractions to their papers if they get new ideas from one another, as long as they can convince each other that the fractions are equivalent.

After they have had a few minutes to talk, reconvene the class and display the Equivalent Fractions on a Clock overhead. Call students' attention to the number in the top corner of each box, and ask them to see if they've found and recorded that many equivalent fractions for each clock on their own sheet. If they come up short on any of the clocks, ask them to work with the people at their table to see if, together, they can generate the missing fractions and add them to their sheets. (If necessary, encourage students to think in terms of halves, thirds, fourths, sixths, twelfths, and sixtieths. While these are certainly not the only equivalents that might be used, they're all relatively easy to find on a clock because each one corresponds with a number shown on the clock face, except for sixtieths, which correspond to the minute marks.)

After they have had a few minutes to work, call on each group to name the fractions for one of the clocks as you record at the overhead. When you've gone around the room once, ask each table to supply the information for another clock until the overhead is complete. As you're recording at the overhead, ask students to record any fractions they hadn't already thought of on their own sheets.

Once all the fractions have been entered on the overhead, ask students to search for patterns. Ask students to pair-share for a few minutes, and then call on volunteers to share their observations with the class. As they share observations, record them on a piece of chart paper. This is meant to be a very open-ended inquiry, and the discussion might go in any number of directions. However, students are likely to mention that some clocks have more fractions than others. Pressing them to explain why this is the case can lead to a discussion of factors and multiples.

> **Students** *Every clock has a fraction with twelfths and a fraction with sixtieths.*
> *We saw that too and we said it's because they all have minutes, so you can talk about sixtieths, and they all have 12 parts because of the 12 numbers, so you can see twelfths on all of them.*
> *There are 4 clocks that only have 2 fractions—the clocks with the minute hand at 1, 5, 7, and 11. It kind of makes sense because those are weird numbers.*

> **Teacher** *How are you thinking about that when you say they're weird, Ariel?*

> **Ariel** *I can't really tell you, except they just don't seem all that friendly. The clocks where the minute hand is on 2, 3, 4, 6, 8, 9, and 12 all have more fractions, and it just seems like those numbers go better with 12 somehow.*

> **Gabe** *I think it has to do with factors, like 2, 3, 4, and 6 are all factors of 12, but 5, 7, and 11 aren't.*

> **Jasmine** *Then how come the first clock doesn't have more fractions? 1 is a factor of 12, right?*

> **Raven** *But you can't do much with 1. I mean, 1 times 12 is 12 and that's that. But on the next clock, it's like you have more going on because you have 1 × 12 is 12 and 2 × 6 is 12.*

End the discussion while student interest is still high. Post the chart of observations, along with the completed Clock Face overhead, and encourage students to add more observations to the chart over the next few days.

Solving Problems and Developing Generalizations
Display only the top portion of the Fractions of an Hour Story Problems overhead while students get out their journals.

Fractions of an Hour Story Problems

1 It takes Zack $\frac{1}{6}$ of an hour to walk to the bus stop and $\frac{2}{6}$ of an hour to get to school once he's on the bus. What part of an hour does it take him to get to school?

2 Alexandra had $\frac{3}{4}$ of an hour to get ready for school this morning. If she had to spend $\frac{1}{4}$ of an hour looking for her shoes, how much time did she have left to do everything else she needed to do to get ready?

Read both problems aloud and work with input from the class to write a matching expression for each problem on the overhead ($^1/_6$ + $^2/_6$ and $^3/_4$ – $^1/_4$) while students do the same in their journals. Ask students to solve one of the problems using their Clock Face Fractions sheet or their fraction kits. Ask them to record their answers in their journals, as well as any sketches or other work they did to solve the problem; if they did it mentally, recording an answer only is fine. Students can choose to work alone or in pairs, and you can ask students who finish quickly and easily to solve both problems. When most have found a solution to at least one of the problems, ask a couple of volunteers to share their solutions and strategies with the class.

> **Theo** *On the first problem, we looked at the clocks on our sheet. $^1/_6$ is 10 minutes and $^2/_6$ is 20 minutes, so it takes Zack 30 minutes to get to school.*

> **Kamil** *But we're supposed to find out what part of an hour it took him, not how many minutes!*

> **Jade** *Well, that's easy. 30 minutes is half an hour. It took him half an hour.*

> **Jaime** *We did it with our fraction strips. We just put $^1/_6$ and then 2 more one-sixths together, and we got three-sixths, but you can see that's the same as $^1/_2$.*

$\frac{1}{6}$	$\frac{1}{6}$	$\frac{1}{6}$
	$\frac{1}{2}$	

> **Ichiro** *For the second problem, we just looked at the clock. We could see that $^3/_4$ – $^1/_4$ left her with half an hour to get ready.*

> **Blanca** *We saw that too, but we also showed it with our fraction strips. We just put out 3 one-fourths, and then took one of them away. It left $^2/_4$, and that's the same as $^1/_2$.*

Then write the answer to each problem to complete the two equations you began at the overhead and examine them with the class. Press students to explain why the numerators have been added or subtracted, but the denominators have not.

$$\frac{1}{6} + \frac{2}{6} = \frac{3}{6} \qquad\qquad \frac{3}{4} - \frac{1}{4} = \frac{2}{4}$$

> **Teacher** *So it seems that we all agree that $^1/_6$ plus $^2/_6$ is $^3/_6$ and $^3/_4 - ^1/_4$ is $^2/_4$, although many of you have noticed that $^3/_6$ and $^2/_4$ are both the same as $^1/_2$ and expressed your answers that way. As I look at our answers, I notice that the numbers along the top, the numerators, have been added or subtracted, but the denominators have not. Why would this be the case? Talk it over with the person next to you, and then let's have a few people share their ideas with the class.*

> **Students** *If you added the denominators on the first one, you'd get $^3/_{12}$, but that doesn't make any sense. If you look on the clock sheet you can see that $^3/_{12}$ is less than $^2/_6$!*
> *If you subtracted the denominators on the second problem, you'd get $^2/_0$. I don't think that's even a real fraction. How can you divide 2 by 0?*
> *I think fractions are kind of like things by themselves. On the first problem, you're adding sixths like you would add $1 + 2$ of anything. You get 3 sixths for an answer.*
> *Yeah, and on the other one, you're subtracting fourths. You have 3 fourths and you get rid of 1 fourth, but everything is still in fourths.*

After some discussion, reveal the prompt below the first two problems and work with student input to write a general statement about adding and subtracting fractions with like denominators. Record the statement at the overhead using students' own words and ideas while students record the statement in their journals.

Overhead 6.4 For use in Unit Six, Session 5.

Fractions of an Hour Story Problems

1 It takes Zack $\frac{1}{6}$ of an hour to walk to the bus stop and $\frac{2}{6}$ of an hour to get to school once he's on the bus. What part of an hour does it take him to get to school?

$$\frac{1}{6} + \frac{2}{6} = \frac{3}{6}$$

2 Alexandra had $\frac{3}{4}$ of an hour to get ready for school this morning. If she had to spend $\frac{1}{4}$ of an hour looking for her shoes, how much time did she have left to do everything else she needed to do to get ready?

$$\frac{3}{4} - \frac{1}{4} = \frac{2}{4}$$

Now reveal problems 3 and 4 at the overhead. Read them out loud, write a matching expression for each on the overhead while students do the same in their journals ($^1/_3 + ^1/_2$ and $^5/_6 - ^1/_4$), and then give them a few minutes to solve one or the other. Ask students who finish quickly to solve both problems and/or challenge them to solve one or the other in two different ways, once using the clock faces and once using the fraction strips. After students have had time to work, invite a few volunteers to share their solutions and strategies with the class.

---

3 After school, Tamara spent $\frac{1}{3}$ of an hour doing her chores and $\frac{1}{2}$ an hour doing her homework. What part of an hour did she spend doing chores and homework?

4 Mr. Taguchi's class went on a field trip to the museum. They were supposed to have $\frac{5}{6}$ of an hour to tour the new dinosaur display, but they had to wait $\frac{1}{4}$ of an hour just to get in. How much time did they have left to see the display?

To add or subtract fractions when the denominators are *different*, you have to:

Darius For the first one, we used the clocks again. $^1/_3$ of an hour is 20 minutes and half an hour is 30 minutes. If you add them up, it's 50 minutes, and that's $^5/_6$ of an hour.

Rian We used our fraction strips. We put $^1/_2$ and $^1/_3$ together, but we couldn't really say what the answer was. Then we saw that if you turn both of the fractions into sixths, you can say that the answer is $^5/_6$.

$\frac{1}{3}$		$\frac{1}{2}$		
$\frac{1}{6}$	$\frac{1}{6}$	$\frac{1}{6}$	$\frac{1}{6}$	$\frac{1}{6}$

Hanako The second one isn't too hard if you do it on the clock. You can see that $^5/_6$ of an hour is 50 minutes, and $^1/_4$ of an hour is 15 minutes. 50 – 15 is 35 minutes, so you can say the answer is $^{35}/_{60}$ or $^7/_{12}$.

Justin We decided to try it with fraction strips and it was kind of hard. We put out $^5/_6$, and tried to figure out how to take away $^1/_4$. We were pretty stuck until Morgan saw that we could turn the sixths into twelfths. Since $^1/_4$ is the same as $^3/_{12}$, we could see that the answer was $^7/_{12}$ then.

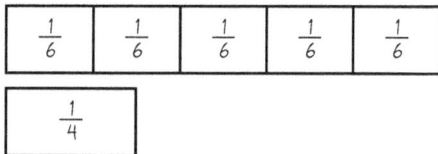

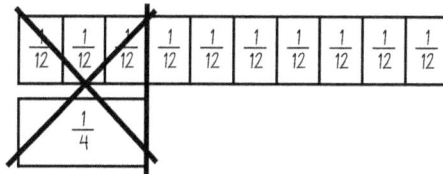

$\frac{1}{6}$	$\frac{1}{6}$	$\frac{1}{6}$	$\frac{1}{6}$	$\frac{1}{6}$

$\frac{1}{4}$

$\frac{1}{12}$	$\frac{1}{12}$	$\frac{1}{12}$	$\frac{1}{12}$	$\frac{1}{12}$	$\frac{1}{12}$	$\frac{1}{12}$	$\frac{1}{12}$	$\frac{1}{12}$

$\frac{1}{4}$

Record the answers to problems 3 and 4 at the overhead and ask students to reflect on them. Record their generalizations on the overhead and ask them to record the generalizations in their journals. Informed by their own experiences and observations, quite a few of your students may already have intuitive understandings about the fact that adding or subtracting fractions with unlike denominators involves renaming them so that they have like denominators. If we add $1/2 + 1/3$, for instance, we can't express the answer until we rename both as sixths (or twelfths or sixtieths). You'll need to make this fact explicit as the class develops and records generalizations by explaining that what they are doing is finding the common denominator, which is the least common multiple, the smallest number that is a multiple of both original denominators. You might pose the following questions to promote discussion.

- How is it possible to have started with a third and a half and ended up with sixths in problem 3? How is it possible to have started with $5/6$ in problem 4, subtracted $1/4$, and ended up with $7/12$?
- Why is it that neither the numerators nor the denominators have been added or subtracted in either problem?
- Whether they used the clocks or the fraction strips, what did students have to do to get the answers to these problems?

$$\frac{1}{3} + \frac{1}{2} = \frac{5}{6} \qquad \frac{5}{6} - \frac{1}{4} = \frac{7}{12}$$

Students *If you added across the top and the bottom, you'd get $2/5$, but that doesn't really make any sense because $2/5$ is less than $1/2$. You can't get less than one of the pieces you started with!*

If you subtracted the numerators and denominators in the other problem, you'd get $4/2$, and that totally doesn't make sense because 4 halves is 2! There's no way you could take something away from $5/6$ and get 2.

It seems like when you add two fractions that are different, you have to change them into things that are alike, and then it's easy. Like with this one, we changed $1/3$ into $2/6$ and $1/2$ into $3/6$, and then we knew that the answer was $5/6$.

And on the other one, as soon as you turn the whole thing into twelfths, it's as easy as the first two problems we did.

Teacher *When you turn them both into things that are alike, as Rian and Justin explained, you're finding a common denominator, that is, a denominator your two fractions could have in common. Then you rename both fractions so they both have that denominator. You have done a good job today of finding common denominators by thinking about common multiples. The smallest common denominator is the least common multiple. The least common multiple is the smallest number that is a multiple of two numbers.*

3 After school, Tamara spent $\frac{1}{3}$ of an hour doing her chores and $\frac{1}{2}$ an hour doing her homework. What part of an hour did she spend doing chores and homework?

$$\frac{1}{3} + \frac{1}{2} = \frac{5}{6}$$

4 Mr. Taguchi's class went on a field trip to the museum. They were supposed to have $\frac{5}{6}$ of an hour to tour the new dinosaur display, but they had to wait $\frac{1}{4}$ of an hour just to get in. How much time did they have left to see the display?

$$\frac{5}{6} - \frac{1}{4} = \frac{7}{12}$$

To add or subtract fractions when the denominators are *different*, you have to:

$$\frac{2}{6} + \frac{3}{6} = \frac{5}{6} \qquad \frac{10}{12} - \frac{3}{12} = \frac{7}{12}$$

Note *When students add and subtract fractions with unlike denominators using fraction strips or clock faces, they search for and find like denominators intuitively. To accomplish this without the models, people often find the least common multiple of both denominators and then multiply the numerator and denominator of each fraction to create equivalent fractions that can be added or subtracted. Given the relative simplicity and compatibility of the fractions fifth graders generally work with, a method this complex doesn't seem warranted. The most important thing for students to take away from this session is the idea that fractions have to be renamed so that they share a common denominator in order to add or subtract them. If you share the idea of finding the first common multiple both denominators share in common, as shown on the overhead above, most students can change thirds and halves to sixths, or sixths and fourths to twelfths, without going through a complicated set of steps, especially if they have fraction strips or clock faces to refer to. If your state requires that fifth graders be proficient at finding common denominators and least common multiples, you might offer some extra practice with this process.*

Solving More Addition and Subtraction Problems

If time remains in the session, write the problems shown below on the whiteboard and ask students to solve all of them in their journals, using the fraction kits or clock face sheets to help if they need them. If students don't have time to finish them during this session, keep them on the board for them to do later today or tomorrow during seatwork.

$$\frac{1}{4} + \frac{1}{3} \qquad \frac{1}{2} + \frac{3}{8} \qquad \frac{2}{6} + \frac{1}{8} \qquad \frac{4}{6} - \frac{3}{12} \qquad \frac{4}{6} - \frac{2}{12} \qquad \frac{5}{6} - \frac{1}{3}$$

Note *Even though students have recorded the generalizations about adding and subtracting fractions in their journals, you'll probably want to transfer these to a chart which you can post for reference in the next session and the rest of the unit. Also, be sure that students will have continued access to their completed Equivalent Fractions on a Clock Home Connections after this session. They can either leave them in their Home Connections Books, or glue them into their Student Journals for future reference.*

Equivalent Fractions on a Clock

2

3

3

4

2

5

2

4

3

3

2

7

Fractions of an Hour Story Problems

1 It takes Zack $\frac{1}{6}$ of an hour to walk to the bus stop and $\frac{2}{6}$ of an hour to get to school once he's on the bus. What part of an hour does it take him to get to school?

2 Alexandra had $\frac{3}{4}$ of an hour to get ready for school this morning. If she had to spend $\frac{1}{4}$ of an hour looking for her shoes, how much time did she have left to do everything else she needed to do to get ready?

To add or subtract fractions when the denominators are the same, you have to:

3 After school, Tamara spent $\frac{1}{3}$ of an hour doing her chores and $\frac{1}{2}$ an hour doing her homework. What part of an hour did she spend doing chores and homework?

4 Mr. Taguchi's class went on a field trip to the museum. They were supposed to have $\frac{5}{6}$ of an hour to tour the new dinosaur display, but they had to wait $\frac{1}{4}$ of an hour just to get in. How much time did they have left to see the display?

To add or subtract fractions when the denominators are *different*, you have to:

Home Connection 50 ★ Worksheet

Equivalent Fractions on a Clock

This clock is broken! The hour hand is stuck at the 12, but the minute hand can still move.

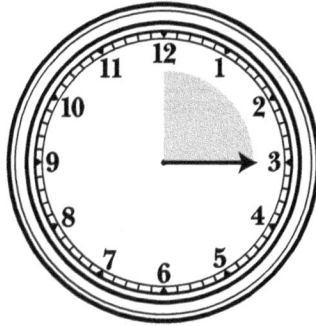

1 Marcus looked at the clock shown above and said, "$\frac{1}{4}$ of an hour has passed." Sierra said, "$\frac{3}{12}$ of an hour has passed." Ali said, "$\frac{15}{60}$ of an hour has passed." Their teacher said they were all correct. Explain how this could be possible.

2 Label each clock with at least 2 equivalent fractions to show what part of an hour has passed. On the clocks marked with stars, write at least 3 equivalent fractions.

a	★b	★c
_____ _____	_____ _____ _____	_____ _____ _____

(Continued on back.)

★d

e

★f

_____ _____ _____

g

★h

★i

_____ _____

★j

k

★l

_____ _____ _____

(Continued on next page.)

Home Connection 50 ★ Activity

Equivalent Fraction Concentration

Use your fraction cards to play a game of concentration with an adult. Here are the instructions:

1 Sort your cards into four piles, and check to be sure there are six cards in each pile. The four piles will be:
- the ones with no mark in the corner
- the star cards
- the lightening bolt cards
- the cards you made

2 Choose two stacks (12 cards in all). Put them together and mix them up. Then lay them out in a 3 × 4 array, face down, like this:

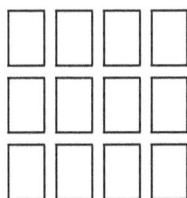

3 Take turns turning two cards face up. If the two cards you get are equivalent fractions, like $\frac{1}{2}$ and $\frac{6}{12}$, you get to keep them. If they're not equivalent, you have to turn them face down again and put them back in exactly the same spot.

4 Each time either player gets a pair of equivalent fractions, you have to explain to the other person how you know they are equivalent. You can use sketches, numbers, or words to do this, and you can help each other.

5 The person with the most cards at the end of the game wins.

6 When you are finished, play the game again with the other two sets of cards, and then have the adult sign the bottom of this page.

⚡ **CHALLENGE**

7 If you want to play a more challenging game, use all 24 of your cards at the same time.

Signature of the adult who played this game with me: _____

© The Math Learning Center

Source: From *Bridges in Mathematics: Grade 5, Teachers Guide* (Vol. 3, pp. 803–811), by R. Deerwater, A. E. Fischer, and A. Fisher, 2007, Salem, OR: The Math Learning Center. Copyright by The Math Learning Center. Reprinted with permission.

Handout 9.1C
Investigating Instructional Materials: Fourth Grade Lesson

Examine the lesson on Handout 9.1A and answer the questions below.

Lesson: *Math out of the Box: Grade 4* (pp. 97–104)

What big ideas, strategies, and mathematical models are being developed in this lesson?
What are the important mathematical concepts underlying the lesson? How does the lesson reflect the concepts from the Common Core State Standards?
What skills and knowledge are required for students to complete the tasks?

Which strands of mathematical proficiency are represented in this lesson?
On pages 147 and 148, the lesson has students adding decimals from left to right and then from right to left. How are these two approaches different? What are the benefits of each approach? How does each approach help students develop procedural fluency?

What are the strengths of this lesson?	What are some limitations, questions, and concerns that you have about the lesson? What misunderstandings and difficulties might your students encounter?

Handout 9.1D
Investigating Instructional Materials: Fifth Grade Lesson

Examine the lesson on Handout 9.1B and answer the questions below.

Lesson: *Bridges in Mathematics: Grade 5* (pp. 803–811)

What big ideas, strategies, and mathematical models are being developed in this lesson?

What are the important mathematical concepts underlying the lesson? How does the lesson reflect the concepts from the Common Core State Standards?

What skills and knowledge are required for students to complete the tasks?

Which strands of mathematical proficiency are represented in this lesson?
How is the lesson designed to help students make sense of adding and subtracting fractions with unlike denominators? What types of questions does the teacher ask students? Which models help illustrate the meanings of the problems?

What are the strengths of this lesson?	What are some limitations, questions, and concerns that you have about the lesson? What misunderstandings and difficulties might your students encounter?

Handout 9.1E

Investigating Your Instructional Materials: Analyzing Lessons

Examine a lesson from your instructional materials that focuses on adding or subtracting fractions or decimals and answer the questions below. You will use your responses to develop the lesson in Session 12.

Lesson: _____   Pages: _____

What big ideas, strategies, and mathematical models are being developed in this lesson?
What are the important mathematical concepts underlying the lesson? How does the lesson reflect the concepts from the Common Core State Standards? What skills and knowledge are required for students to complete the tasks?
What are the similarities and differences between this lesson and the sample lesson from Handout 9.1A or 9.1B?

Which strands of mathematical proficiency are represented in this lesson?	
What are the strengths of this lesson?	**What are some limitations, questions, and concerns that you have about the lesson?** **What misunderstandings and difficulties might your students encounter?**

Handout 9.2A

Mathematics Games: Adding and Subtracting Fractions and Decimals

Beat the Clock

Materials: Handout 9.2B: Beat the Clock Recording Sheets (one copy prepared for each player) and Handout 9.2C Beat the Clock Fraction Cards (cut out from three copies of handout on cardstock)

Groups: To be played in groups of two to four students

Directions:

- One player shuffles the fraction cards and turns six cards faceup on the table.

- Each card represents a fraction of an hour.

- The object of the game is for each player to use any number of the six cards to get as close to one whole hour without going over.

- When players are finished, they verify each other's answers and determine the winner for the round.

- Play continues for at least four rounds.

Variation: The object of the game is to use any number of cards to get as close to zero as possible. The recording sheet would include the following open number sentence

$$1 - \underline{\qquad} - \underline{\qquad} - \underline{\qquad} - \underline{\qquad} - \underline{\qquad} - \underline{\qquad} - \underline{\qquad} - \underline{\qquad} = \underline{\qquad}$$

❖ ❖ ❖

Estimating Sums

Materials: Handout 9.2D Estimating Sums Game Cards (cut out from one copy of Handout 9.2D on colored cardstock), and Handout 9.2E Estimating Sums Fraction Cards (cut out from one copy of Handout 9.2E on a second color of cardstock)

Groups: To be played in groups of two or three students

Directions:

- Each player gets one of each estimation game card: 0, ½, 1, 1½, 2, and 2½.

- Fraction cards are placed facedown in one pile on the table.

- For each round, take the top two cards from the pile of fraction cards and put them faceup on the table.

- Players each estimate the sum of the two fractions and place one of their estimation game cards (0, ½, 1, 1½, 2, and 2½) that they think is closest to the sum.

- After all players have placed their estimation card, they calculate and come to consensus on the actual sum.

- The first player to put down the closest estimation card collects the fraction cards. If players put down the correct card at exactly the same time, they share the fraction cards.

- Players retrieve their estimation game cards.

- Play continues until there are no more fraction cards.

- The player with the most fraction cards wins the game.

Variation: Play with decimal numbers or combine fraction and decimal cards.

❖ ❖ ❖

Take Five

Materials: Handout 9.2F One Hundredth to One Chart, Handout 9.2G Take Five Decimal Cards (cut out from three copies of Handout 9.2G on cardstock), 10 clear chips to cover numbers on the chart, and one game piece for each player

Groups: To be played in groups of two students

Directions:

- The object of the game is to "take" a chip. If a player's game piece lands on the same number as a chip, the player gets to take the chip. Players can only take one chip on any given turn. The player who is the first to take five chips wins the game.

- Together, players place 10 clear chips on the One Hundredth to One Chart.

- Players each place their game piece on any empty space on the One Hundredth to One Chart.

- One player shuffles decimal cards and gives five cards to each player.

- Remaining cards are placed facedown in one pile on the table.

- Players choose who will have the first turn.

- On each turn, players each may use one to five of their cards to move to another space on the chart. Players will each move their game piece by adding or subtracting the amount indicated on their card(s).

- Used cards are placed in a discard pile.

- At the end of a turn, players take enough cards from the pile so they have five cards.

- If a player runs out of cards before play ends, one player shuffles the cards from the discard pile and places them facedown in a pile on the table.

Variation: More clear chips can be added to include more players.

❖   ❖   ❖

Close to Two

Materials: Handout 9.2H Close to Two Grids for each player, Handout 9.2I Close to Two Spinners, paper clip, and pencils

Groups: Two to four players

Directions:

- One Close to Two grid is distributed to each player. Each ten-by-ten grid represents one whole.

- The spinner works by holding the paper clip in place in the center of the spinner using a pen or pencil. Players spin the paper clip while holding the pencil still.

- The object of the game is to get closest to two, without going over, after three spins.

- For each round, players take turns using the spinner to determine the amount to shade on their ten-by-ten grid on their individual Close to Two handout. On each turn, a player must be able to shade in the whole amount indicated on the spinner on one ten-by-ten grid. If there is not enough space, the player loses a turn.

- After three rounds, players calculate who is closest to two without going over.

- The player closest to two without going over wins the game.

Variation: Game can be played with the fraction spinner.

❖   ❖   ❖

High Five

Materials: Handout 9.2J High Five Cards (cut out from one copy of Handout 9.2J on cardstock), and Handout 9.2K High Five Recording Sheet

Groups: Two to four players

Directions:

- One player shuffles the number cards, zero through nine, and places the pile facedown on the table.

- Each player receives two decimal points, one addition symbol, and one equal sign.

- To play a round, players each take four number cards. Using their individual number cards, decimal points, addition symbol, and equal sign, the players each create two numbers whose sum is as close to five as possible without going over.

  Example:

4	.	1	+	.	6	5	=

- Players record their number sentence and the sum on their individual High Five Recording Sheets. In this example, the sum is .25 away from 5.

- The player with a sum closest to five without going over wins the round. Players can use models or tools—such as calculators, base-ten blocks, money, and number lines—to help them calculate this amount.

Variations: Players could receive three decimal points, two addition signs, and one equal sign. Or players could receive three decimal points, one addition sign, one subtraction sign, and one equal sign.

Handout 9.2B
Beat the Clock Recording Sheet

_____ + _____ + _____ + _____ + _____ + _____ + _____ + _____ = _____

_____ + _____ + _____ + _____ + _____ + _____ + _____ + _____ = _____

_____ + _____ + _____ + _____ + _____ + _____ + _____ + _____ = _____

Beat the Clock Fraction Cards

$\dfrac{1}{2}$	$\dfrac{1}{3}$	$\dfrac{1}{4}$	$\dfrac{1}{5}$
$\dfrac{1}{6}$	$\dfrac{1}{10}$	$\dfrac{1}{12}$	$\dfrac{1}{15}$
$\dfrac{1}{20}$	$\dfrac{1}{30}$	$\dfrac{1}{60}$	$\dfrac{2}{3}$
$\dfrac{3}{4}$	$\dfrac{2}{5}$	$\dfrac{3}{5}$	$\dfrac{4}{5}$
$\dfrac{5}{12}$	$\dfrac{7}{12}$	$\dfrac{2}{15}$	$\dfrac{3}{20}$

Estimating Sums Game Cards

0	0	0	0
$\frac{1}{2}$	$\frac{1}{2}$	$\frac{1}{2}$	$\frac{1}{2}$
1	1	1	1
$1\frac{1}{2}$	$1\frac{1}{2}$	$1\frac{1}{2}$	$1\frac{1}{2}$
2	2	2	2
$2\frac{1}{2}$	$2\frac{1}{2}$	$2\frac{1}{2}$	$2\frac{1}{2}$

Estimating Sums Fraction Cards (page 1)

$\dfrac{1}{2}$	$\dfrac{2}{2}$	$\dfrac{1}{3}$	$\dfrac{2}{3}$
$\dfrac{3}{3}$	$\dfrac{1}{4}$	$\dfrac{2}{4}$	$\dfrac{3}{4}$
$\dfrac{4}{4}$	$\dfrac{1}{5}$	$\dfrac{2}{5}$	$\dfrac{3}{5}$
$\dfrac{4}{5}$	$\dfrac{5}{5}$	$\dfrac{1}{6}$	$\dfrac{2}{6}$
$\dfrac{3}{6}$	$\dfrac{4}{6}$	$\dfrac{5}{6}$	$\dfrac{6}{6}$

Estimating Sums Fraction Cards (page 2)

$\dfrac{1}{8}$	$\dfrac{2}{8}$	$\dfrac{3}{8}$	$\dfrac{4}{8}$
$\dfrac{5}{8}$	$\dfrac{6}{8}$	$\dfrac{7}{8}$	$\dfrac{8}{8}$
$\dfrac{1}{10}$	$\dfrac{2}{10}$	$\dfrac{3}{10}$	$\dfrac{4}{10}$
$\dfrac{5}{10}$	$\dfrac{6}{10}$	$\dfrac{7}{10}$	$\dfrac{8}{10}$
$\dfrac{9}{10}$	$\dfrac{10}{10}$	$\dfrac{1}{12}$	$\dfrac{2}{12}$

Estimating Sums Fraction Cards (page 3)

$\dfrac{3}{12}$	$\dfrac{4}{12}$	$\dfrac{5}{12}$	$\dfrac{6}{12}$
$\dfrac{7}{12}$	$\dfrac{8}{12}$	$\dfrac{9}{12}$	$\dfrac{10}{12}$
$\dfrac{11}{12}$	$\dfrac{12}{12}$	$\dfrac{1}{100}$	$\dfrac{2}{100}$
$\dfrac{3}{100}$	$\dfrac{4}{100}$	$\dfrac{5}{100}$	$\dfrac{10}{100}$
$\dfrac{20}{100}$	$\dfrac{25}{100}$	$\dfrac{50}{100}$	$\dfrac{75}{100}$

Handout 9.2F
One Hundredth to One Chart

.01	.02	.03	.04	.05	.06	.07	.08	.09	.1
.11	.12	.13	.14	.15	.16	.17	.18	.19	.2
.21	.22	.23	.24	.25	.26	.27	.28	.29	.3
.31	.32	.33	.34	.35	.36	.37	.38	.39	.4
.41	.42	.43	.44	.45	.46	.47	.48	.49	.5
.51	.52	.53	.54	.55	.56	.57	.58	.59	.6
.61	.62	.63	.64	.65	.66	.67	.68	.69	.7
.71	.72	.73	.74	.75	.76	.77	.78	.79	.8
.81	.82	.83	.84	.85	.86	.87	.88	.89	.9
.91	.92	.93	.94	.95	.96	.97	.98	.99	1

Handout 9.2G

Take Five Decimal Cards

+ .01	+ .01	+ .02	+ .03
− .01	− .01	− .02	− .03
+ .1	+ .2	+ .3	− .11
− .1	− .2	− .3	− .12
+ .11	+ .12	+ .13	− .13

Close to Two Game Grids

Game 1

_____ + _____ = _____

I am _____ away from two.

Game 2

_____ + _____ = _____

I am _____ away from two.

Close to Two Spinners

Decimal Spinner

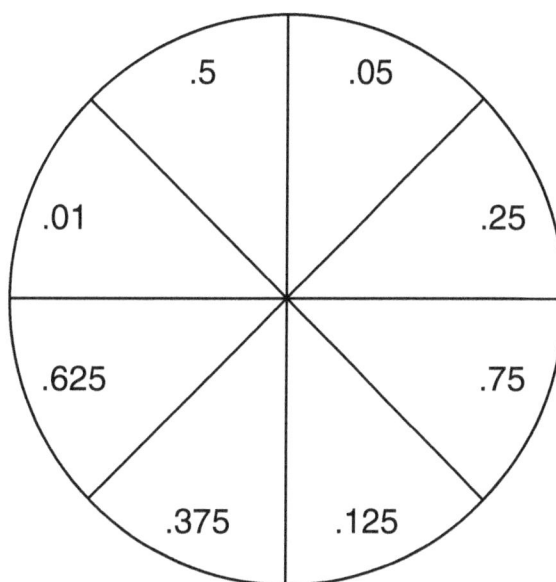

Fraction Spinner

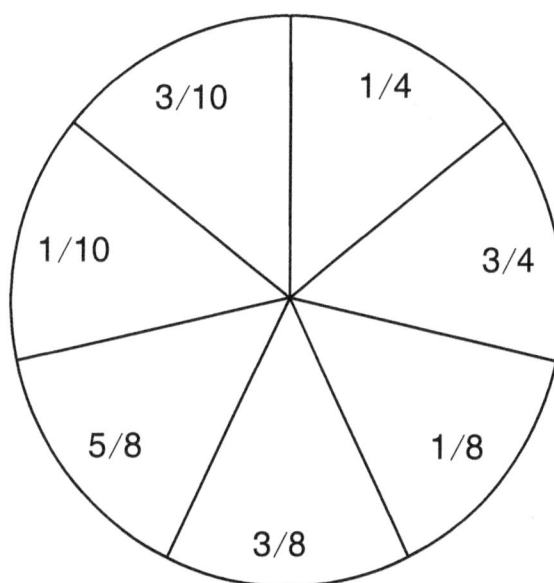

High Five Cards (page 1)

0	1	2	3
4	5	6	7
8	9	0	1
2	3	4	5
6	7	8	9

High Five Cards (page 2)

●	●	●	●
●	●	●	●
+	+	=	=
0	1	2	3
4	5	6	7

Handout 9.2K
High Five Recording Sheet

Round One

_____ + _____ = _____ My sum is _____ away from 5.

Round Two

_____ + _____ = _____ My sum is _____ away from 5.

Round Three

_____ + _____ = _____ My sum is _____ away from 5.

Round Four

_____ + _____ = _____ My sum is _____ away from 5.

Round Five

_____ + _____ = _____ My sum is _____ away from 5.

Handout 9.4

Student Connections: Observing Children Playing Games

Select at least one of the games from Activity 9.2 to play with one small group of children. Write detailed notes below describing the strategies each student uses while solving a problem during the game.

Student 1	
Describe game situation and strategy.	
Student 2	
Describe game situation and strategy.	
Student 3	
Describe game situation and strategy.	

Session 10

Understanding Standard Procedures

What are the important mathematical concepts that underlie each step of the standard procedures for adding and subtracting fractions and decimals?

Description

In the previous sessions, you have been exploring ways to help children develop conceptual understanding of the addition and subtraction of fractions and decimals using models, games, and flexible strategies for finding equivalent expressions. In this session, you will examine the standard procedures (algorithms) for adding and subtracting fractions and decimal numbers and uncover the mathematical concepts that underlie these procedures.

Key Ideas

- Understanding the mathematical concepts that underlie the steps in standard procedures for adding and subtracting fractions and decimals can help students develop proficiency and fluency.

- Identifying students' common errors in calculation can provide valuable information to guide a teacher's instructional decisions.

- A landscape of learning that maps strategies, big ideas, and mathematical models can help teachers understand where their students are heading as they move into more advanced mathematics.

Outline of Activities

- 10.1: Analyzing Student Connections: Mathematics Games   (15 minutes)
- 10.2: Common Errors With Standard Procedures   (15 minutes)
- 10.3: Concepts That Support Efficient Procedures With Rational Numbers   (30 minutes)
- 10.4: Landscape of Learning   (20 minutes)
- 10.5: Before the Next Session   (5 minutes)
- 10.6: Lesson Design Notes   (5 minutes)

What to Bring

- Notes and student work: Student Connections activities (Handouts 2.4 and 9.4)
- Handout 4.4 from previous sessions
- Common Core State Standards: Standards for Mathematical Content

To Complete Before Session 11

- Student Connections: Addition and Subtraction With Fractions and Decimals (Handout 10.5)

Facilitator Notes   Session 10

Understanding Standard Procedures

If this is your first time facilitating the group, please refer to the more detailed facilitator guidelines in the Introduction. As the facilitator, it is generally your job to keep the conversation flowing and watch the clock. Use your judgment to decide when it's appropriate to extend a session for good conversation or when it's time to move on to the next activity. Remember to keep the group norms posted and revise them, as a group, as necessary.

Before the Session

- Make copies of the following handouts for each team member:
    - ☐ 10.3 Standard Procedures for Addition and Subtraction of Rational Numbers
    - ☐ 10.4 Landscape of Learning: Fractions, Decimals, and Percents
    - ☐ 10.5 Student Connections: Addition and Subtraction With Fractions and Decimals
- Gather the following materials to be used in this session:
    - ☐ Group norms (from Activity 1.4)
    - ☐ Chart paper
    - ☐ Markers
- Remind team members to bring the following items from previous sessions:
    - ☐ Journal (and writing instruments)
    - ☐ Completed homework, Handout 2.4 Student Connections: Adding and Subtracting Fractions and Decimals, and Handout 9.4 Student Connections: Observing Children Playing Games
    - ☐ Handout 4.4 Common Core State Standards
    - ☐ Common Core State Standards: Standards for Mathematical Content

During the Session

- Post group norms, and revise as a group as necessary.
- Activity 10.1: facilitate discussion and sharing.
- Activity 10.2: facilitate discussion.
- Activity 10.3: facilitate discussion; facilitate partnering, if necessary; serve as recorder.

After the Session

- Remind team members of homework, Handout 10.5 Student Connections: Addition and Subtraction With Fractions and Decimals
- Pass any team materials to the next facilitator.

Activity 10.1 Analyzing Student Connections: Mathematics Games

15 minutes   Handout 9.4 Student Connections: Observing Children Playing Games

Your task from Session 9.4 was to select one of the games from Activity 9.2 to play with a small group of students and to record your observations on Handout 9.4.

Read your completed Student Connections activity, Handout 9.4, and the notes you wrote in your journal.

Share with your group the approaches your students used.

Discuss the following questions:

- Which game did you select and why?

- What strategies did children use to play each game? Was there anything that surprised you?

- What evidence was there that the game supported children in developing a conceptual understanding of addition and subtraction with decimals and fractions?

- After watching your students play the game, how would you change or adapt the game to provide challenges at an appropriate level to meet the needs of all of your students?

Write in your journal about new insights you have about your students after this activity. What new questions do you have about developing conceptual understanding and skill in adding and subtracting decimals and fractions? What new tasks or questions might help you to find out more about their thinking? What instructional strategies might help the struggling students you interviewed?

Activity 10.2 Common Errors With Standard Procedures

15 minutes   Handout 2.4 Student Connections: Adding and Subtracting Fractions and Decimals

Computing with rational numbers (fractions and terminating or repeating decimals) involves applying procedures that can seem complex. Helping students develop fluency with adding and subtracting fractions and decimals has proven to be quite challenging for many teachers. In this activity, you will examine some common errors that students typically make when computing with fractions and decimals and consider instructional moves that can help students overcome these errors.

Read and discuss each of the errors listed below that students may make when adding and subtracting with fractions and decimals. While you are working, use the following questions to guide your discussion about each error:

- Describe the error. What step in the procedure is misapplied? Why would this lead to an incorrect answer?

- Is this a common error you find your students making? Did you note evidence of this error in the Student Connections activity, Handout 2.4?

- Why do students make this type of error?

- When your students make this error, how do you help them understand why this process doesn't work?

- What are some questions that you could ask to help the student identify the error and understand the reasoning needed in order to correct the error?

a. $\dfrac{1}{4} + \dfrac{2}{3} = \dfrac{3}{7}$

b. $1.7 + .25 = .42$

c. $4.5 - .33 = 1.2$

d. $6\dfrac{1}{3} - 1\dfrac{2}{3} = 4\dfrac{9}{3}$

6 1/3
− 1 2/3
4 9/3

5 11/3
− 1 2/3
4 9/3

Review the results of the Student Connections activities on Handout 2.4.

Discuss any other errors that your students make when computing with fractions and decimals.

Activity 10.3 Concepts That Support Efficient Procedures With Rational Numbers

30 minutes

Handout 10.3 Standard Procedures for Addition and Subtraction With Rational Numbers

Students often find it challenging to add and subtract fractions and decimals without making errors. Teachers also often find it frustrating to teach students procedures that are useful for computing efficiently. The standard procedures for adding and subtracting fractions and decimals include many steps that students often find difficult to remember. In fact, students often lose the meaning of the fractional values when they focus exclusively on these procedures. In this activity, your group will discuss the steps in some standard procedures for addition and subtraction with rational numbers. You will then connect them to several key mathematical concepts that underlie and support the steps in the procedures that are vital to helping students develop fluency with these operations.

Complete the problems in the first column on both sides of Handout 10.3 Standard Procedures for Addition and Subtraction With Rational Numbers. As you do so, describe each step in the procedure you are using.

Compare your work with the work of a team member, using the following questions:

- Did you use the same steps to solve the problems? If not, discuss the differences.
- Read the accompanying procedural descriptions you wrote. Did you describe the process the same way as your partner?

Discuss your responses with the rest of the group. It might be helpful to create a group list of steps for common procedures on chart paper.

Read the following list of mathematical concepts:

Mathematical Concepts That Support the Addition and Subtraction of Rational Numbers

1. Each place in the base-ten number system is related by powers of 10. In other words, places moving to the left are valued 10 times the previous place, places to the right are valued one-tenth the previous place. Any place "without" a value can be filled with a 0.

2. One conceptualization of a fraction is a number that can be used to represent part of a whole or part of a set. In this representation, the denominator indicates the number of equal parts in the whole or set, and the numerator indicates the number of parts being described.

3. The sum of or difference between two fractions can be expressed as a single fraction only when the parts are of the same size. The sum of or difference between two decimals can be expressed as a single number only when the parts are of the same size.

4. Two fractions are equivalent if they are representations for the same amount, quantity, portion, or ratio. Equivalent fractions can be found by applying the identity property of multiplication: The product of any number and 1 is the number itself. For example, $6 \times 1 = 6$ or $\frac{3}{4} \times 1 = \frac{3}{4}$. The value of 1 can be written in many forms. For example, $1 = \frac{2}{2}$, $1 = \frac{7}{7}$, or $1 = \frac{x}{x}$. Therefore, if you multiply a fraction by the value of one, the result will be an equivalent fraction. For example, $\frac{2}{3} \times \frac{3}{3} = \frac{6}{9}$ or $\frac{a}{b} = \left(\frac{a}{b}\right) * 1$.

Match each step of the list you created on Handout 10.3 with one or more of the mathematical concepts in the preceding box. What are the important concepts that underlie each step within the standard procedures?

Record your findings in the right-hand column.

Discuss the following questions:

- How does the number of steps in the procedures compare with the number of underlying mathematical concepts in the problems?

- Students often make errors when following the steps in standard procedures. This may be attributed to moving too quickly to standard procedures without sufficient time spent on developing conceptual understanding. Do you agree or disagree with this statement? Is it the teachers or the students who are moving too fast?

- How might paying attention to what are often referred to as "careless errors" help uncover underlying patterns of errors that are related to a particular mathematical concept?

- What implications does a focus on steps in procedures have on instructional decisions?

- What implications does a focus on mathematical concepts have on instructional decisions?

Connect each step of the common procedures you listed as a group to one or more of the mathematical concepts.

Activity 10.4 Landscape of Learning

20 minutes

Handout 4.4 Common Core State Standards
Handout 10.4 Landscape of Learning: Fractions, Decimals, and Percents
Common Core State Standards: Standards for Mathematical Content

In Session 2, you started brainstorming components of a learning landscape for fractions and decimals. This tool is based on the idea of teachers developing a map that describes how students typically progress in their mathematical understanding. This big picture lays out what is most important for students to learn and many routes that students might take to get there.

In several sessions, you have added to your components of a learning landscape (Handout 2.3 in your journal). We will now connect your ideas to the work of Dolk and Fosnot, who use the term *landscape of learning* to describe the progression of student thinking in mathematics. The following quotation illustrates their approach.

> The metaphor of a landscape suggests a picture of a learning terrain in which students move in meandering or direct ways as they develop strategies and ideas about mathematical topics. Along students' journeys there are moments of uncertainty, moments of potential shifts in understanding (crossroads), and moments where mathematical ideas or strategies are constructed (landmarks). Knowledge of these moments gives teachers the capacity to better understand, document, and stretch students' thinking.
>
> Maarten Dolk and Catherine Twomey Fosnot (2006),
> *Fostering Children's Mathematical Development:*
> *The Landscape of Learning* (p. vii)

Handout 10.4 is the landscape of learning for fractions, decimals, and percents. This is the model developed by Dolk and Fosnot. You will be looking more closely at three domains of the landscape: strategies, big ideas, and mathematical models. In this activity, the term *landscape of learning* refers to the map on Handout 10.4; the term *components of a learning landscape* refers to the web of ideas that you have been developing on Handout 2.3.

Keep in mind that the landscape of learning on Handout 10.4 was developed to represent student learning related to fractions and decimals from fourth grade through sixth grade. For this reason, Dolk and Fosnot's diagram includes strategies, big ideas, and models that are further along in the landscape than those at which children typically arrive in fourth or fifth grade. However, it can be helpful for teachers to understand where their students are heading as they move into more advanced mathematics.

The landscape of learning is intended to be read from bottom to top. That is, the information contained at the lower portion of the map describes basic or early strategies, big ideas, and models. As you move up the page, closer to the "horizon" depicted with a cityscape, you will see listed strategies, big ideas, and models that are more advanced or sophisticated.

Strategies

Read and highlight the strategies on Handout 10.4, which are contained within rectangles on the landscape of learning.

Discuss the following questions:

- Compare the strategies on the Dolk and Fosnot landscape with the strategies you included on your components web. What similarities and differences can you identify? Is there anything your group would like to add to your components web?

- In your experience, which strategies are typical for fourth grade? Which strategies are typical for fifth grade? Which strategies are more likely to emerge in the sixth grade?

Big Ideas

Read and highlight the big ideas on Handout 10.4, which are contained within the ovals on the landscape of learning.

Discuss the following questions:

- Compare the big ideas on the Dolk and Fosnot landscape with the big ideas you included on your components web. What similarities and differences can you identify? Is there anything your group would like to add to your components web?

- In your experience, which big ideas are typically addressed in fourth grade? Which big ideas are typically addressed in fifth grade? Which big ideas are more likely to be addressed in the sixth grade?

Mathematical Models

Read the mathematical models on Handout 10.4, which are contained within the triangles on the landscape of learning.

Discuss the following questions:

- Compare the models on the Dolk and Fosnot landscape with the models you included on your components web. What similarities and differences can you identify? Is there anything your group would like to add to your components web?
- In your experience, which models are typically used in fourth grade? Which models are typically used in fifth grade? Which models are more likely to be appropriate in sixth grade?

Compare the landscape of learning to the Common Core State Standards (see Handout 4.4 and Standards for Mathematical Content for your grade level).

Discuss the following questions:

- What connections do you see between the landscape of learning and the sequence of learning objectives in the Common Core State Standards?
- What are the differences?
- Are there ideas from the Common Core State Standards that you want to add to your components web?

Reflect and write responses to the following in your journal:

- How could the landscape of learning help you to organize your knowledge about how your students learn mathematics?
- How can it help you to plan lessons and assess where students are in their mathematical development?
- How might it help you locate students who are on different "roads"?
- Do you recognize particular "landmarks" in student learning?
- How might the "map" help the struggling student catch up with the capable student?
- How might it continue to challenge the capable student?

Share your responses with your group members.

Activity 10.5 Before the Next Session

5 minutes

Handout 10.5 Student Connections: Addition and Subtraction
With Fractions and Decimals

Handout 10.5 is an activity that you can use in your classroom to collect updated information about your students' knowledge of addition and subtraction with fractions and decimals. Before the next session, and without prior instruction, ask your students to complete the addition and subtraction problems on the handout. These are the same problems you explored in

Activity 10.3. Encourage them to make their explanations as detailed as possible. As your class is working, select one student who typically struggles with mathematics and one student who typically catches on more quickly. Observe how they work on and solve the problems. Write down your observations in your journal. Collect all student work when they are finished. You will examine this student work in the next session.

Bring your students' completed Student Connections activity, Handout 10.5, to the next session.

Activity 10.6 Lesson Design Notes

5 minutes

The key ideas for this session are

- Understanding the mathematical concepts that underlie the steps in standard procedures for addition and subtraction with fractions and decimals can help students develop proficiency and fluency with the standard procedures.

- Identifying students' common errors in calculation can provide valuable information to guide a teacher's instructional decisions.

- A landscape of learning that maps strategies, big ideas, and mathematical models can help teachers understand where their students are heading as they move into more advanced mathematics.

Reflect on what you learned during this session and how the ideas apply to each of the three themes in your Lesson Design Notes. A few prompts related to the themes follow. These are merely suggestions and should not limit your reflection or the ideas you capture.

- Where do you want to go?
  - In Activity 10.4, you examined the landscape of learning for fractions and decimals. What are the connections between the landscape of learning and your goals for students' mathematical learning?

- Where are you now?
  - How does the landscape of learning help you understand where your students are in developing their mathematical knowledge? What ideas of the landscape of learning are relevant to the notes you have captured so far?
  - In Activity 10.2, you identified common errors students make when using standard procedures for adding and subtracting fractions and decimals. Which of these errors have you seen your students make? How can you help students understand the source of these errors?

- What is the best way to get there?
  - In Activity 10.3, you explored concepts that support efficient procedures with rational numbers. How will you use these mathematical concepts to inform your instructional decisions? What types of activities or lessons could you develop to help your students build understanding of these concepts?

References and Resources

Barnett, C., Goldenstein, D., & Jackson, B. (Eds.). (1994). *Fractions, decimals, ratios, and percents: Hard to teach and hard to learn?* Portsmouth, NH: Heinemann.

Dolk, M., & Fosnot, C. T. (2006). *Fostering children's mathematical development: The landscape of learning* [CD-ROM]. Portsmouth, NH: Heinemann.

Fosnot, C. T., & Dolk, M. (2002). *Young mathematicians at work: Constructing fractions, decimals, and percents.* Portsmouth, NH: Heinemann.

Jacob, B., & Fosnot, C. T. (2007). *Best buys, ratios, and rates: Addition and subtraction of fractions.* Portsmouth, NH: Heinemann.

Kilpatrick, J., Swafford, J., & Findell, B. (Eds.). (2001). *Adding it up: Helping children learn mathematics.* Washington, DC: National Academies Press.

Lamon, S. J. (1999). *Teaching fractions and ratios for understanding.* Mahwah, NJ: Lawrence Erlbaum.

Standard Procedures for Addition and Subtraction With Rational Numbers

Problem & Steps	Description of Steps in the Procedure	Mathematical Idea or Property
$\dfrac{1}{4} + \dfrac{3}{8}$		

Problem & Steps	Description of Steps in the Procedure	Mathematical Idea or Property
$1\dfrac{1}{4} - \dfrac{2}{3}$		

Problem & Steps	Description of Steps in the Procedure	Mathematical Idea or Property
$65.4 - 13.08$		

Problem & Steps	Description of Steps in the Procedure	Mathematical Idea or Property
$\dfrac{1}{3} + .4$		

Landscape of Learning: Fractions, Decimals, and Percents

FRACTIONS, DECIMALS, and PERCENTS

uses fractions, decimals, and percents interchangibly

fractions, decimals, and percents as rational numbers

fractions, decimals, and percents as operators

interchanging numerators to simplify first when multiplying

doubling and halving and the more generalized use of the associative property to eliminate a fraction

standard algorithms

ratio table for division

the properties that hold for whole number operations also hold for rational numbers

using landmark fractions to make partial products

open array model for multiplication

constant rate can be determined if the accumulated rate and time are known

simplifies to make a common whole

multiplication and division of rational numbers are relations on relations

accumulated increase of a constant rate is the rate times the time

use of double number line for addition and subtraction

fractions may represent a rate

using place value understanding to multiply and divide by powers of ten

using a common whole to add and subtract fractions

generalized use of a repertoire of strategies for whole number operations

skip counting or using repeated add to find a fraction of a whole

fractions can be thought of as operators

clock model

using the associative property to make "friendly" numbers and adjusting at the end

uses money as landmark numbers

using landmark decimals

if the whole is shifted one can work with decimals using whole-number arithmetic

to add or subtract fractions a common whole is needed

equivalence is preserved when equivalent parts are combined

uses multiplication and division to make equivalent fractions

using repeated addition for multiplying

multiplication and division by ten make the whole shift to the right and to the left in a decimal representation

using a ratio table as a tool to make equivalent fractions

counting on instead of removal in subtraction

ratio table

using proportional reasoning

doubles numerator and denominator to make equivalent fractions

if numerators are common only denominators matter when comparing

equivalence on a double number line

with decimal equivalences the numbers in different place-value positions are related by powers of ten

doubles numerator to multiply by two

doubles a denominator to halve a fraction

for equivalence the ratio must be kept constant

uses a common whole to compare fractions

to compare fractions the whole must be the same

multiplication is connected to fractions (e.g. 3/4 = 3 x 1/4)

fair sharing

pieces don't have to be congruent to be equivalent

measurement

fraction bars

analog electric meter

fractions express relationships the size or amount of the whole matters

fractions may represent division with a quotient less than one

with unit fractions, the greater the denominator, the smaller the piece is

money model

using landmark percentages (e.g. 50%)

using landmark fractions (e.g. 1/2, 1/4)

using landmark decimal equivalents

The landscape of learning: fractions, decimals, and percents on the horizon showing landmark strategies (rectangles), big ideas (ovals), and models (triangles).

Handout 10.5

Student Connections: Addition and Subtraction With Fractions and Decimals

Find the solution. Be sure to show all of your work, including pictures that show your thinking.

$\dfrac{1}{4} + \dfrac{3}{8}$
$1\dfrac{1}{4} - \dfrac{2}{3}$
$65.4 - 13.08$
$\dfrac{1}{3} + .4$

Session 11

Instruction to Support Fluency With Standard Procedures

What are the important ideas to consider when designing instruction for addition and subtraction of rational numbers?

Description

In the previous session, you explored several mathematical concepts that support students in developing fluency with addition and subtraction of fractions and decimals. In this session, you will examine your students' work and consider their level of understanding with these concepts and fluency with standard procedures. Your group will consider how this information can be used to design your instruction.

Key Ideas

- Understanding the mathematical concepts that support the standard procedures for addition and subtraction with fractions and decimals can help teachers design learning experiences for students.

- Identifying students' common errors can provide valuable information to guide a teacher's instructional decisions.

- The design of the prototype lesson is based on teachers' knowledge of student learning, content, and instruction.

- An understanding of the unit and how concepts develop within a unit is important when planning a lesson.

Outline of Activities

- 11.1 Analyzing Student Connections   (15 minutes)
- 11.2 Instruction for Standard Procedures   (15 minutes)
- 11.3 Prototype Lesson Template   (10 minutes)
- 11.4 Lesson Design: Three Themes   (25 minutes)
- 11.5 Mapping the Unit   (25 minutes)

What to Bring

- Handouts from previous sessions (4.4, 6.3, and 10.4)
- Notes and student work: Student Connections activity (Handout 10.5)
- Notes and student work: previous Student Connections activities (Handouts 2.4, 3.4, 6.4, 7.4, and 9.4)
- Investigating Instructional Materials activities (Handouts 7.3A–E, 9.1A–E and NCTM Illuminations activity with notes)
- Common Core State Standards: Standards for Mathematical Content

Facilitator Notes   Session 11

Instruction to Support Fluency With Standard Procedures

If this is your first time facilitating the group, please refer to the more detailed facilitator guidelines in the Introduction. As the facilitator, it is generally your job to keep the conversation flowing and watch the clock. Use your judgment to decide when it's appropriate to extend a session for good conversation or when it's time to move on to the next activity. Remember to keep the group norms posted and revise them, as a group, as necessary.

Before the Session

- Make copies of the following handouts for each team member:
    - ☐ 11.3 Prototype Lesson: Overview
    - ☐ 11.5 Unit Map Template
- Gather the following materials to be used in this session:
    - ☐ Group norms (from Activity 1.4)
    - ☐ Chart paper
    - ☐ Markers
    - ☐ Unit plans or outlines (addition and subtraction) from different curricula, if available
- Remind team members to bring the following items from previous sessions:
    - ☐ Journal (and writing instruments)
    - ☐ Handouts 4.4, 6.3, 7.3A–E, 9.1A–E, and 10.4
    - ☐ Notes and student work, Student Connections activities (Handouts 2.4, 3.4, 6.4, 7.4, 9.4, and 10.5)
    - ☐ Common Core State Standards: Standards for Mathematical Content

During the Session

- Post group norms, and revise as a group as necessary.
- Activity 11.1: facilitate discussion and sharing.
- Activity 11.2: facilitate discussion.
- Activity 11.4: facilitate discussion; serve as recorder.
- Activity 11.5: facilitate discussion; serve as recorder.

After the Session

- Pass any team materials to the next facilitator, including charted notes from Activity 11.3.

Activity 11.1 Analyzing Student Connections

15 minutes

Handout 10.5 Student Connections: Addition
and Subtraction With Fractions and Decimals

In Session 10, you examined the standard procedures for adding and subtracting with fractions and decimals and several mathematical concepts that support these standard procedures. Your group will now examine the Student Connections activity (Handout 10.5) that was assigned in the last session.

Read your completed Handout 10.5 Student Connections from Session 10. Think about the mathematical concepts that support the addition and subtraction of fractions and decimals in Activities 10.3 and 10.4. How can you use these ideas to describe the extent of your students' conceptual understanding of addition and subtraction with fractions and decimals?

Discuss the following questions with a partner:

- How did your students solve the equations? Did they use standard procedures? Did they use other strategies? What key ideas did they understand?
- Describe the errors that your students made. For what key ideas do they seem to lack understanding?
- Which students appear to have a conceptual understanding of fractions and decimals? How do you know? Describe the evidence.
- Is there anything that surprised you after reading your students' work? How will you use the ideas from this discussion to inform your next instructional decisions?

Share your discussion with the rest of the group.

Activity 11.2 Instruction for Standard Procedures

15 minutes

Helping children develop fluency with standard procedures is a primary focus for many teachers. The traditional approaches to teaching might not provide adequate experiences for students to develop understanding of the key ideas that are critical to developing fluency.

Discuss the following questions with your group:

- What are your thoughts about the placement of standard procedures in a learning sequence? Should they serve as a starting point or should we use them as an extension to learning, after students develop conceptual understanding of addition and subtraction with fractions and decimals?
- Do you find it difficult to help students become fluent with standard procedures? What makes this topic difficult to teach?
- Generate a list of some of the "problems" or challenges associated with helping your students become successful with standard procedures.

Consider the following (simulated) teacher-researcher exchanges. Which of these dialogues relate to the problems or challenges you listed?

❖   ❖   ❖

Teacher: There is always so much to cover, yet so little time. I don't know how I can fit it all in. How can I spend a significant amount of time on fraction and decimal concepts when I have to make sure my students can add and subtract with fractions and decimals?

Researcher: Instruction on computing with rational numbers has traditionally centered on memorizing algorithms or rules. A lesson may include the teacher demonstrating a procedure for solving a type of problem, followed by students practicing this procedure on a worksheet with many similar problems. However, researchers have found that this type of instruction is overreliant on memorization and does not support conceptual understanding. (Kilpatrick, Swafford, & Findell, 2001)

❖   ❖   ❖

Teacher: If students have to learn the standard procedures, isn't it easiest to show them how to follow the steps and give them enough practice so they commit it to memory? This is how I learned fractions when I was in fifth grade. I don't know how to do it any other way.

Researcher: Studies have indicated that instruction focusing solely on memorizing and practicing procedures has little impact on helping students understand computation with rational numbers. Following such instruction, less than half of the students interviewed in one study were able to add fractions correctly. Even fewer students were able to explain how to add fractions. Traditional algorithms do not usually correspond with students' understanding of the operations and the meaning they demonstrate through drawings and manipulatives. Instructional programs that provide real-life problems and honor students' invented strategies help build a conceptual understanding of computation with rational numbers. Guiding classroom discussions on students' approaches to these problems facilitates the development of increasingly efficient algorithms. (Kilpatrick et al., 2001)

❖   ❖   ❖

Teacher: My students are supposed to start studying fractions and decimals in earlier grades before they come to my class. They play with the manipulatives then. By the fourth and fifth grade, we need to get down to business and work on the symbolic notation and algorithms.

Researcher: Based on the research, the recommendation is for instruction to focus on developing students' conceptual understanding. Classroom activities that build on students' knowledge of fractions, use appropriate models and manipulatives, and are embedded in real-life contexts help students construct meaning of the operations. It is imperative for students to not only understand the key ideas behind each operation, but also to make explicit connections between these ideas and the procedural rules in algorithms. (Kilpatrick et al., 2001)

❖ ❖ ❖

Discuss the following questions with your group:

- Which of these teacher concerns relates to a topic you discussed? What is your response to the researchers' comments?

- What problems did you list that were not addressed in these dialogues? How do you think one of these researchers might respond?

Write a response to the following question in your journal:

- What additional questions do you now have about helping students develop fluency with standard procedures?

Activity 11.3 Prototype Lesson Template

10 minutes   Handout 11.3 Prototype Lesson: Overview

In Session 12, you will use all the work you have done so far to develop a collaboratively designed prototype lesson. The purpose of the lesson is to put the knowledge and ideas you have generated into practice and to find out what the results are for students.

Read the following description of the prototype lesson.

The lesson you develop in this session of the *Teaching by Design* process is not intended to be perfect. Instead, the purpose is for you to have the experience of drawing on the group's shared expertise to craft a lesson that considers long- and short-term goals, important mathematical ideas, and appropriate instructional practices, all matched with the needs of students. The purpose also includes testing your ideas and hypotheses and revising based on what actually happens. This should lead to a new or deeper understanding. The prototype lesson is also an opportunity to gather data to address questions or hypotheses about student learning and to try out new ideas.

It is not necessary to start from scratch to design the prototype lesson. You may choose to start with an activity from your instructional materials or from the other instructional materials that you reviewed in previous sessions. Your team will add to this framework and adapt it so that you can enact the ideas related to the work you have been doing.

Review your copy of Handout 11.3 Prototype Lesson: Overview. It is intended to provide an overview of the content and format for designing a lesson. During the rest of this session, you will begin identifying ideas and questions that will inform the design of the prototype lesson. Keep the template in mind as you engage in the next two activities.

Activity 11.4 Lesson Design: Three Themes

25 minutes

Handout 4.4 Common Core State Standards
Handout 6.3 Five Strands of Mathematical Proficiency
Handout 10.4 Landscape of Learning
Investigating Instructional Materials activities (Handouts 7.3A–E, 9.1A–E, and NCTM Illuminations activity)
Student Connections activities (Handouts 2.4, 3.4, 6.4, 7.4, 9.4, and 10.5)
Common Core State Standards: Standards for Mathematical Content

In this activity, you will review your notes, handouts, and other materials from previous sessions. The purpose of this process is to identify the information and ideas that you have collected throughout the sessions. These ideas will guide the process of designing your prototype lesson in Session 12.

The broad content area of the prototype lesson will be fractions or decimals. The discussions in this activity are intended to help you hone in on the specific mathematical concepts for the prototype lesson.

Much of the information that you need for this activity will be captured in your Lesson Design Notes. However, the other handouts and materials may be helpful if you find that you need more information about a particular idea or question.

Gather and briefly review your Lesson Design Notes (Handout 1.3 in your journal). Keep the other handouts and notes on hand for reference.

Scan the questions that follow and identify the ones that you believe have a high priority. You may not have time to discuss all of the questions in depth, so start with the questions that will help generate the most ideas. You should try to discuss questions related to all three *Teaching by Design* themes.

Discuss the questions and **record** your ideas on chart paper.

Where are we now?

- What do the results of the Student Connections activities tell us about our students?
- What are students' experiences with the number and operations concepts stated in the Common Core State Standards?
- What are students' strengths when it comes to these concepts?
- In what areas do students need support with these concepts?

Where do we want to go?

- What are our long-term goals for students?
- How are these goals related to the five strands of mathematical proficiency?
- How do your goals for students relate to the Common Core State Standards?
- Where do our students need to go next on the learning landscape?

What is the best way to get there?

- What mathematical concepts from the Common Core State Standards should our lesson address?
- What are the big ideas, strategies, and mathematical models associated with these concepts?
- What ideas from our investigations of instructional materials should we consider including in the lesson?

Informed by the ideas in your team's discussion, you will now select the mathematical concepts that will be addressed in your team's prototype lesson.

Identify the mathematical concept(s) that will serve as the focus of your team's prototype lesson and record it on the chart paper.

You will have additional opportunities to review your notes and discuss these questions as you plan the prototype lesson. Be sure to bring the chart paper notes to Session 12.

Activity 11.5 Mapping the Unit

25 minutes   Handout 11.5 Unit Map Template

In the previous activity, you identified the mathematics concepts that the prototype lesson will address. An understanding of how this lesson fits within a larger unit and how concepts develop within a unit is important when planning a lesson. Through the process of mapping or unit planning, you will gain a strong understanding of how each lesson fits with other lessons, and how skills and understanding of concepts develop.

Create an outline of the unit for the topic that you have identified. Handout 11.5 provides a template for this map of the unit. If your instructional materials include an outline in which the goals, mathematical concepts, and activities are described for each lesson, use this document as a starting point for the unit map.

It can be helpful to examine how different units on the same topic are sequenced in different curricula. If possible, compare your outline with other units that focus on the concepts for the unit you are mapping.

Discuss the following questions:

- How do your instructional materials address the topic you have selected?
- Which concepts does each lesson in the unit address?
- Are there sufficient opportunities for students to work on these ideas?
- Based on your work in previous sessions, do the lessons provide appropriate experiences that reflect how students learn?
- How are the lessons sequenced in the unit?
- What are the goals of the unit? What will students understand by the end of the unit?
- Which concepts are missing in the unit?

Revise the sequence of the unit as necessary. There may be changes that you identify in the flow of the lessons, such as revising the order in which certain strategies or concepts are presented. (This is an optional step that may not be necessary for the unit you have selected.)

Identify the lesson within the unit that you will collaboratively design as your team's prototype lesson. Consider the following questions in order to make your decision:

- Which lesson will have the most impact on the unit?
- Which lesson is the most challenging to teach?
- Why should we focus on this lesson?
- What will students learn in the activities leading up to the lesson?
- Where will they be going next?

In the next session, you will collaborate on designing the prototype lesson. Gather all the chart paper and other notes that you generated during this session. Be sure to bring all the relevant materials—see the overview page of Session 12 for a list.

References and Resources

Dolk, M., & Fosnot, C. T. (2006). *Fostering children's mathematical development: The landscape of learning* [CD-ROM]. Portsmouth, NH: Heinemann.

Fosnot, C. T., & Dolk, M. (2002). *Young mathematicians at work: Constructing fractions, decimals, and percents.* Portsmouth, NH: Heinemann.

Kilpatrick, J., Swafford, J., & Findell, B. (Eds.). (2001). *Adding it up: Helping children learn mathematics.* Washington, DC: National Academies Press.

Handout 11.3
Prototype Lesson: Overview

Design Team: [The team of teachers who designed the lesson]

Teacher: [The team member who teaches the prototype lesson]

School: **Grade Level:**

Title: [Descriptive name for the lesson]   **Date:**

Where are we now?

Background Information

[This section describes the research that the team conducted to design the prototype lesson and describes students' current understanding of the targeted mathematical concepts and skills.]

Where do we want to go?

[This section identifies the goals and outcomes that shape the details and design of the lesson.]

Unit Goals

[The broad goals of the unit in which the lesson occurs.]

Learning Outcomes

[The expected outcomes of the prototype lesson.]

Sequence of the Unit

[This section describes where the prototype lesson occurs in the unit, including the lessons that occur prior to the prototype lesson and those that occur after.]

Lesson 1	
Lesson 2	
Lesson 3	
Lesson 4	
Lesson 5	

Evaluation and Data Collection

[This section describes the specific data that will be collected during the teaching of the prototype lesson to determine the extent to which the goals and learning outcomes of the lesson were met.]

What is the best way to get there?

Lesson Outline

[This section describes the flow of the lesson in detail.]

Learning Activities and Teacher Questions	Expected Student Responses	Teacher Support
[This column identifies what students will be doing and how the teacher will set up and facilitate the tasks.]	[This column describes how the team anticipates how students will respond to the tasks and teacher questions.]	[This column describes how the teacher will respond to the anticipated reactions from students.]

Handout 11.5
Unit Map Template

Title:

Title or Topic of the Lesson	Goal and Learning Activities

Session **12**

Designing the Prototype Lesson

Overview

How can we use what we know about important mathematical concepts, student learning, and effective instructional elements to design a lesson?

Description

In this session, you will work collaboratively to develop the prototype lesson. Your group will use the ideas you have collected in your learning landscapes, what you have learned about your students, your understanding of the mathematical concepts from the Common Core State Standards, and your existing instructional materials to inform the design.

Key Ideas

- Teachers' research on pedagogy and student learning influences the design and content of a lesson.
- The purpose of creating a collaboratively designed prototype lesson is to improve instruction by generating professional knowledge, not by developing an exemplary lesson.

Outline of Activities

- 12.1 Overview of the Prototype Lesson Sessions
- 12.2 Background Information
- 12.3 Goals and Learning Outcomes
- 12.4 Evaluation and Data Collection
- 12.5 Lesson Process

Note: It is likely that it will take more than one session to design the lesson. Estimated times are not included for this session because the amount of time needed for the activities will vary.

What to Bring

- Handouts from previous sessions (4.4, 6.3, 10.4, 11.3, and 11.5)
- Common Core State Standards: Standards for Mathematical Content
- Notes and student work: Student Connections (Handouts 2.4, 3.4, 6.4, 7.4, 9.4, and 10.5)
- Investigating Instructional Materials activities (Handouts 7.3A–E, 9.1A–E, and NCTM Illuminations activity with notes)

To Complete Before Session 13

- Teach and observe the prototype lesson.

Facilitator Notes   Session 12

Designing the Prototype Lesson

If this is your first time facilitating the group, please refer to the more detailed facilitator guidelines in the Introduction. As the facilitator, it is generally your job to keep the conversation flowing and watch the clock. Use your judgment to decide when it's appropriate to extend a session for good conversation or when it's time to move on to the next activity. Remember to keep the group norms posted and revise them, as a group, as necessary.

Before the Session

- Make copies of the following handouts for each team member:
  - ☐ 12.2 Prototype Lesson: Template
- Gather the following materials to be used in this session:
  - ☐ Group norms (from Activity 1.4)
  - ☐ Charted notes from Activity 11.4
  - ☐ State mathematics standards or benchmarks
- Remind team members to bring the following items from previous sessions:
  - ☐ Journal (and writing instruments)
  - ☐ Handouts 4.4, 6.3, 10.4, 11.3, and 11.5
  - ☐ Common Core State Standards: Standards for Mathematical Content
  - ☐ Notes and student work, Student Connections activities (Handouts 2.4, 3.4, 6.4, 7.4, 9.4, and 10.5)
  - ☐ Investigating Instructional Materials activities (Handouts 7.3A–E, 9.1A–E, and NCTM Illuminations activity with notes)

During the Session

- Post group norms, and revise as a group as necessary.
- Activity 12.1: facilitate discussion.
- Activity 12.3: lead brainstorming, and serve as recorder of ideas.
- Next Steps activity: facilitate scheduling of lesson teaching

After the Session

- Pass any team materials to the next facilitator.

Activity 12.1 Overview of the Prototype Lesson Sessions

The next three sessions will focus on designing, teaching, observing, discussing, and revising the prototype lesson. Before you start developing the lesson plan, it may be helpful to decide how you are going to collect information about the implementation of the lesson. Collecting data about student learning is an important step in determining the impact of the prototype lesson and in identifying ideas that can inform future lessons. You will be using the data to discuss the lesson in Session 13 and to revise the lesson in Session 14.

There are several different ways that teams of teachers can engage in this process:

Lesson study: One team member will volunteer to teach the lesson to his or her students and the other team members will observe the students. The team may choose to invite others to observe the lesson as well. The observers take detailed notes about what students do and say and report their findings back to the team. The advantage of having multiple observers is the ability to collect data on multiple groups of students.

Peer observation: Two teachers can pair up to observe the lesson in each other's classrooms. As in lesson study, the focus will be on collecting data on the students rather than observing the teacher.

Video study: Each team member will videotape the students as they engage in the lesson and review the tapes independently to observe student learning. It can be especially rich if each person identifies a brief segment to share with the whole group during the discussion of the prototype lesson.

Coaching: The coach will observe the lesson in the teachers' classrooms, focusing on students. It is also possible that the coach will teach the lesson and the teachers will observe. The coach and the teacher(s) will share the data after the lesson.

If you will not be doing live observations or using video it will be challenging to collect the data that you need for Sessions 13 and 14. If this is the only option, take as many notes as possible as you teach the lesson. Focus on a few students rather than trying to record everything that happens. It may be helpful to look at the discussion questions for Session 13 in order to identify the data that you will discuss. As soon as possible after the lesson, sit down and record as much as you can about what students said and did. In addition, analyze the student work. Identify the observations and examples that you want to share with the team in Session 13.

Discuss the options for collecting data and decide on the best strategy for your team.

Activity 12.2 Background Information

Handout 11.3 Prototype Lesson: Overview
Handout 11.5 Unit Map Template
Handout 12.2 Prototype Lesson: Template
Student Connections activities (Handouts 2.4, 3.4, 6.4, 7.4, 9.4, and 10.5)
Common Core State Standards: Standards for Mathematical Content
Chart paper notes from Activity 11.4

In this session, you will be using all the work you have done so far to develop a collaboratively designed prototype lesson using Handout 12.2 Prototype Lesson: Template. The notes that you have taken during previous sessions will serve as an important starting point for planning a lesson together. The materials listed are all resources that might be related to the goals and outcomes of the lesson. However, it is not necessary to consult all these notes and handouts, just the ones that are useful for your team.

Record the information for your design team, teacher, school, grade level, and date on Handout 12.2. You may find it helpful to refer to Handout 11.3 Prototype Lesson: Overview that includes a brief description of each section of the prototype lesson template.

The Background Information section of the lesson template provides a place to write about the research you did in preparation for designing the lesson. It is a place to make connections between the important mathematical concepts underlying the lesson and unit; the Common Core State Standards; the big ideas, strategies, and mathematical models in the learning landscape; your knowledge of student understanding; and your experience with instructional materials and strategies.

Develop and record the background information for the prototype lesson on Handout 12.2. To help you identify the information to include, you may want to consider the following questions. Select the questions that are most helpful or interesting to you—it is not necessary to answer all of them.

- Why was this lesson selected?

- How did you choose the learning activities in the lesson?

- Where does this lesson fall within the learning landscape?

- What Common Core State Standards are being addressed?

- What strand of mathematical proficiency is being addressed?

- Why is it important to have this lesson at this particular time in students' learning?

- What are the key instructional strategies needed for this lesson?

- What evidence of student learning will you collect?

Activity 12.3 Goals and Learning Outcomes

Handout 4.4 Common Core State Standards
Handout 6.3 Five Strands of Mathematical Proficiency
Handout 11.5 Unit Map Template
Investigating Instructional Materials
(Handouts 7.3A–E, 9.1A–E, and NCTM Illuminations activity)
Common Core State Standards: Standards for Mathematical Content
Chart paper notes from Activity 11.4

Sequence of the Unit

The Sequence of the Unit section of the lesson plan template describes the instructional progression, including what students have learned prior to the prototype lesson and what their next steps will be. This section should refer to the unit map that you created in Session 11 (Handout 11.5).

Record the unit map in Sequence of the Unit on Handout 12.2. You can provide a summary in this section, or attach the handout to the lesson plan.

To get started on the lesson, you will identify goals and outcomes to shape the details and design of the lesson. You should consider both unit goals, which may have been developed in the unit-planning phase—the overall goals for the unit within which the prototype lesson is located—and the lesson's expected outcomes for specific student learning.

Unit Goals

You may have identified or developed goals during Activity 11.5. Unit goals are usually broader than a lesson's expected outcomes and long-term in nature. For mathematics, there are sometimes two different types of unit goals. A content goal identifies the specific concepts or understandings. A process goal identifies the strategies, skills, or habits of mind that students will develop. You may find it helpful to refer to the five strands of mathematical proficiency (Handout 6.3) and the Common Core State Standards: Standards for Mathematical Practice (Handout 4.4) when identifying the process goals for the unit. Some examples of content and process goals are listed in the following table.

Unit Goals	
Content	*Process*
Students will understand that in order to add and subtract fractions, there must be a common whole and the denominators must be the same.	Students will develop flexible strategies for finding equivalent fractions to help them add and subtract fractions with unlike denominators.

Discuss the goals you have listed in your notes from Activities 11.4 and 11.5. Did you identify both content and process goals? How do these goals align with your state standards, Common Core State Standards, strands of mathematical proficiency, and learning landscape? What adaptations are needed to make the goals appropriate for the prototype lesson?

Record the goals for the unit on Handout 12.2 Prototype Lesson: Template.

Learning Outcomes

The learning outcomes of your lesson should be directly related to the unit goals, but more specific. They serve as criteria for determining lesson effectiveness. The learning outcomes will help you decide what data to collect during the teaching of the lesson, as well as your discussion of the lesson after it has been taught (Session 13). Some examples of learning outcomes are listed in the following table.

Unit Goals		Learning Outcomes
Content	Process	
Students will understand that in order to add and subtract fractions, there must be a common whole and the denominators must be the same.	Students will develop flexible strategies for finding equivalent fractions to help them add and subtract fractions with unlike denominators.	Students will use number lines to represent and find equivalent fractions. Students will use a clock model to represent and find equivalent fractions. Students will use numerical reasoning to find a common denominator for adding or subtracting fractions with unlike denominators.

Brainstorm possible learning outcomes for the prototype lesson. Are these learning outcomes closely related to the goals of the unit? What skills and knowledge will be developed in this lesson?

Record the expected learning outcomes for the lesson on Handout 12.2 Prototype Lesson: Template.

Activity 12.4 Evaluation and Data Collection

The Evaluation and Data Collection section of the lesson template describes the specific data that will be collected when teaching the prototype lesson, and allows the team to determine the extent to which the goals and learning outcomes of the lesson were met. A key consideration in designing the prototype lesson is what you will have students doing so that learning is visible. The team should collect and review any written work produced by students during the lesson as well as any observer notes (what the teacher said, what students said and did) during their discussion and analysis of the lesson (Session 13). It is often helpful to have students work in pairs or small groups because the teacher and other observers can listen to student conversations. This is especially true when producing written work, which may be time-consuming and challenging for students.

Discuss what would convince the design team that the expected outcomes of the lesson were met.

- What kinds of data will help us assess students' progress toward the goals and learning outcomes?
- What work will students produce? What will this work tell us about student thinking?
- How will we check for understanding?
- What guiding questions will you provide observers to focus collection of data?

Record the specific types of data that will be collected during the lesson in the Data Collection section of Handout 12.2. Data may include written student work, characteristics of student discussion, students' strategies, teacher questions, displays, and so on. Some examples of potential data sources are listed in the box below. It is a good idea to return to this section once you have finished designing the lesson to make sure that the data sources you have listed are appropriate and that your list is complete.

Data Collection

1. Observers will collect data.
   - What types of strategies did students use?
   - What confusion or misconceptions surfaced for students?
   - How are students using the manipulatives?
   - How are students keeping track of their solutions?
2. Student work will be collected and analyzed.
   - What does students' written work reveal about their understanding of the problem or areas of confusion?
   - How do students' drawings provide information about the strategies they used?

Activity 12.5 Lesson Process

The Lesson Process section of the prototype lesson plan template describes the flow of the lesson in detail and includes three components:

- Learning activities and teacher questions
- Expected student responses
- Teacher support

Learning Activities and Teacher Questions

The first column outlines the learning activities and teacher questions—what students will be doing and how the teacher will set up and facilitate the tasks. This part of your lesson plan should be clear enough for someone who was not involved in the planning of the lesson to envision what will happen throughout the lesson. It is also often helpful to estimate how much time each phase of the lesson will take.

The learning activities and teacher questions column describes important points for the teacher to remember in setting up the learning activities, such as allowing time for student discussion. You should describe how the teacher and students will use the board or other visual aids during the lesson. The questions that the teacher will pose to students should be determined ahead of time and included in this section. As much as possible, consider the wording of the questions and prompts from the perspective of your students.

Develop and record the learning activities and teacher questions on Handout 12.2. The following questions may help you as you complete this column:

- How will the lesson be introduced?
- What activities follow?
- How will the lesson end?
- Does the flow of the lesson make sense?
- How will the goals and learning outcomes be made explicit for students?
- What are the main questions that students will explore?
- How will the activities be scaffolded to meet the needs of all students?
- What materials will be needed?

Example:

Learning Activities and Teacher Questions	Expected Student Responses	Teacher Support
Launch: *We just finished working on using the number line to help us find some equivalent fractions.* *I'd like you to look at this clock. What are some things that you know about clocks?* *Today, you are going to work with your partners on these two questions:* 1. *What are all the fractions that can be easily represented using the face of a clock?* 2. *What equivalent fractions can be easily represented using the face of a clock?*		

Expected Student Responses

The second column describes expected student responses to the learning activities and teacher questions. Consider the data that you have collected with the Student Connections activities, as well as the learning landscape, as you insert items into this column.

In order to generate possible student responses it is important to do the activities or tasks yourselves, keeping your students in mind. You may try out several different activities before you decide on the most effective one(s). Doing the activities in this way can also help you to identify potential difficulties that students may encounter with the content or learning activities. In addition, try to identify prior knowledge and potential misconceptions that the students will bring to the lesson.

Develop and record the expected student responses on Handout 12.2. Consider the range of students that you have in your class. The following questions may help you to complete this column:

- What will students think and do in response to each of the instructional activities?
- How might students respond to the questions?
- What strategies might students use?
- What answers might they give?
- When is it okay—or even desirable—for students to be confused?

Example:

Learning Activities and Teacher Questions	Expected Student Responses	Teacher Support
Launch: *We just finished working on using the number line to help us find some equivalent fractions.* *I'd like you to look at this clock. What are some things that you know about clocks?*	• "They are used to tell time." • "They have numbers on them." • "There are twelve numbers." • "They have an hour hand." • "There are 24 hours in a day." • "There's a.m. and p.m." • "Between the numbers on the clock, there are also 5 little spaces." • "There are 60 little spaces in all."	
Today, you are going to work with your partners on these two questions: *1. What are all the fractions that can be easily represented using the face of a clock?* *2. What equivalent fractions can be easily represented using the face of a clock?*	• "We found halves and twelfths. See, you can divide the clock in half if you draw an imaginary line down the clock from the 12 to the 6. That would be halves. Then there are also 12 spaces between the 12 numbers. That would be twelfths. We found that $\frac{1}{2}$ is equal to $\frac{6}{12}$." • "We found quarters and halves. My mom is always saying 'it's a quarter after' or 'a quarter to.' If you draw a vertical line from 12 to 6 and a horizontal line from 9 to 3, you get fourths. We found that $\frac{2}{4}$ is equal to $\frac{1}{2}$. Also that four fourths, or $\frac{4}{4}$, is equal to one whole."	

Teacher Support

The third column—teacher support—describes how the teacher will respond to the anticipated responses from students. This includes questions that the teacher can pose to extend student thinking or to help students reevaluate their misconceptions. It can provide a contingency plan to enact if students struggle.

This section also provides thinking questions that the teacher can pose to students as they are working. You may want to list things to look for to identify the strategies that students are using or the ideas they are discussing. This will help the teacher to facilitate the closing of the lesson by identifying the students to call on or by anticipating how to bring new ideas into the discussion.

Develop and record your ideas for the Teacher Support section on Handout 12.2. The following questions may be of help as you complete this column.

- How can student misconceptions and confusion be addressed?
- What questions will further student understanding?
- What supports are necessary to provide access for all learners?
- How will the teacher help students who are struggling or frustrated?
- How will the teacher continue to challenge students who quickly finish the task?
- How can we rephrase the questions if students do not respond?
- How can we make the task more or less complex without undermining the goal?

Example:

Learning Activities and Teacher Questions	Expected Student Responses	Teacher Support
Launch: *We just finished working on using the number line to help us find some equivalent fractions.* *I'd like you to look at this clock. What are some things that you know about clocks?*	• "They are used to tell time." • "They have numbers on them." • "There are twelve numbers." • "They have an hour hand." • "There are 24 hours in a day." • "There's a.m. and p.m." • "Between the numbers on the clock, there are also 5 little spaces." • "There are 60 little spaces in all."	*If I look over here at the 1, how many spaces are there between the 12 and 1?* (5) *If I look over here at 3, how many spaces are there between the 12 and 2?* (10) *If I look over here at 4, how many spaces are there between the 12 and 3?* (15) *What pattern do you notice?* (counting by fives)
Today, you are going to work with your partners on these two questions: 1. *What are all the fractions that can be easily represented using the face of a clock?* 2. *What equivalent fractions can be easily represented using the face of a clock?*	• "We found halves and twelfths. See, you can divide the clock in half if you draw an imaginary line down the clock from the 12 to the 6. That would be halves. Then there are also 12 spaces between the 12 numbers. That would be twelfths. We found that $\frac{1}{2}$ is equal to $\frac{6}{12}$." • "We found quarters and halves. My mom is always saying 'it's a quarter after' or 'a quarter to.' If you draw a vertical line from 12 to 6 and a horizontal line from 9 to 3, you get fourths. We found that $\frac{2}{4}$ is equal to $\frac{1}{2}$. Also that four fourths, or $\frac{4}{4}$, is equal to one whole."	*Distribute copies of clocks printed on transparency sheets to groups of students. Ask them to record their findings on the sheets.* *Distribute large index cards and ask students to write down equivalent fractions.* *Using the overhead projector, ask students to share the fractions found. Place transparencies on top of one another and ask students to describe the relationship between different fractions, for example, sixths and twelfths.* *Post the completed index cards on the board and ask students to sort them by fractions with related denominators.*

Next Steps

When the design of the prototype lesson is complete, the next step is to teach it in one or more classrooms and to gather data. The prototype lesson template will serve as the guide for teaching the lesson. It is important to stay as close as possible to the prototype plan. When you observe the lesson, either in the classroom or on video, you will use the plan to collect data.

If you are using observations in the classroom, it will be very important for the observers to stay focused on students rather than the teacher. Your data collection should include detailed notes about what students are doing and saying throughout the lesson. Observers should refer to the Evaluation and Data Collection section of the completed prototype lesson.

The next session will focus on discussing the results of the prototype lesson. The following artifacts will inform the discussion of the prototype lesson:

- Observation notes
- Video
- Student work
- Photos of any visual displays
- Teacher reflections

Handout 12.2
Prototype Lesson: Template

Design Team:

Teacher:

School: Grade Level:

Title: Date:

Where are we now?

Background Information

Where do we want to go?

Unit Goals

Learning Outcomes

Sequence of the Unit

Lesson 1	
Lesson 2	
Lesson 3	
Lesson 4	
Lesson 5	

Evaluation and Data Collection

1.

2.

3.

What is the best way to get there?

Lesson Outline

Learning Activities and Teacher Questions	Expected Student Responses	Teacher Support

Session 13

Discussing Results

What does the evidence tell us about the impact of our lesson on student learning?

Description

The focus of this stage of the *Teaching by Design* process is on discussing the implementation of the prototype lesson and reviewing evidence about student learning. When engaging in a structured discussion process, the team identifies how students responded to each component of the lesson. This discussion serves as the basis for the lesson revision in Session 14.

Key Ideas

- Using multiple sources of data provides a reliable way to assess student learning.
- Collecting and examining data on student learning can inform teachers about the effectiveness of a lesson.

Outline of Activities

- 13.1 Reporting on the Lesson   (30 minutes)
- 13.2 Analyzing the Evidence   (60 minutes)
- 13.3 Review and Preview   (5 minutes)

What to Bring

- Copies of the prototype lesson
- Data collected during the teaching of the lesson, which might include students' written work, teachers' observation notes, teachers' reflections, video, or photos of any visual displays

235

Facilitator Notes   Session 13

Discussing Results

If this is your first time facilitating the group, please refer to the more detailed facilitator guidelines in the Introduction. As the facilitator, it is generally your job to keep the conversation flowing and watch the clock. Use your judgment to decide when it's appropriate to extend a session for good conversation or when it's time to move on to the next activity. Remember to keep the group norms posted and revise them, as a group, as necessary.

Before the Session

- Make copies of the following handouts for each team member:
  - ☐ 13.2A Analyzing the Evidence: Data Sources
  - ☐ 13.2B Analyzing the Evidence: Learning Outcomes and Goals
- Gather the following materials to be used in this session:
  - ☐ Group norms (from Activity 1.4)
- Remind team members to bring the following items from previous sessions:
  - ☐ Journal (and writing instruments)
  - ☐ Handout 12.2 Prototype Lesson: Template
  - ☐ Copies of the prototype lesson
  - ☐ Notes and data collected during the lesson

During the Session

- Post group norms, and revise as a group as necessary.
- Activity 13.1: help group adhere to guidelines, and serve as timekeeper.
- Activity 13.2: serve as recorder.

After the Session

- Pass any team materials on to the next facilitator.

Activity 13.1 Reporting on the Lesson

30 minutes

Copies of the prototype lesson
Notes from teaching or observing the lesson
Data collected while observing the lesson

In the time since your last session, one or more teachers from your team taught the *Teaching by Design* prototype lesson. In this session, you will describe what happened during the lesson and analyze the data collected during the teaching, with a focus on understanding how the lesson influenced student learning. Before you begin this process, review the group norms that were developed in Session 1.

The teacher (or teachers) who taught the lesson will provide an overview of what happened.

It is important to observe the following guidelines during this process:

- There should be no interruptions from others.

- Listeners should write down any questions they have and ask them at the end of the teacher's presentation.

- Everyone in the group should have a copy of the lesson plan.

Teacher Report

The teacher(s) who taught the lesson should address the following questions (no more than 10 minutes):

- How did the lesson go?

- How did students respond to each part of the lesson?

- What components of the lesson plan were helpful while teaching?
    - Learning activities and teacher questions
    - Expected student responses
    - Teacher support

- Were there any surprises or unexpected student reactions?

- Were there any aspects of the lesson plan from which you deviated?
    - If so, how and why did you decide to deviate from the plan?
    - What were the results of this decision?

- Based on observations of student learning, what questions would you like the team to address in the next activity, after everyone has had a chance to share their observations?

If your team is using video study, each teacher may also show a clip during the discussion.

Observer Reports

If other team members were able to observe the lesson, they can now share highlights and important points from their notes (approximately 20 minutes). The emphasis in their comments should be on student learning and the implications of those comments for the design of the lesson. The purpose of the observer's report is not to evaluate or critique the teacher. If you are discussing more than one teaching and observation, consider the commonalities and differences between the episodes.

Observers discuss the following questions:

- What evidence of student learning did you see?

- Were there any surprises or unanticipated student responses? Misconceptions?

- Based on your observations related to student learning, what questions do you have about the lesson?

Activity 13.2 Analyzing the Evidence

60 minutes

Handout 13.2A Analyzing the Evidence: Data Sources

Handout 13.2B Analyzing the Evidence: Learning Outcomes and Goals

Copies of the prototype lesson

In this activity, you will be analyzing the evidence gathered during the teaching of the lesson as it relates to the goals and expected outcomes in the lesson. The discussion should include evidence collected from all of the classes in which the lesson was taught. If one group member taught the lesson while others observed, the evidence will be from one class. If the lesson was taught in multiple classes, the evidence from all of the classes will be examined (and additional time might be needed).

During this process, it is helpful to remember that the purpose of developing the prototype lesson in *Teaching by Design* is not to create a perfect lesson, but to have the experience of drawing on the group's shared expertise to craft a lesson that considers long- and short-term goals, important mathematical ideas, and appropriate instructional practices—all matched with the needs of students. This session will give you the opportunity to examine the evidence of student learning collected during the teaching and decide if students have met the goals of the lesson.

It is also helpful to remember that, as teachers, we sometimes are afraid of hurting the feelings of a group member and, as a result, comments and data analysis may only focus on the positive. It's important for teams to look closely at all of the evidence of student learning when deciding on the success of a lesson. The discussion should include both the strengths and weaknesses of the lesson based on the evidence of student learning.

It is important to note that certain mathematical concepts may take many lessons for students to build knowledge. An effective lesson does not always equate with all students accurately solving a given task with ease. A lesson can still be effective if students are building understanding of a concept.

Handouts 13.2A and 13.2B provide tools for capturing the results of this analysis. Your team should select the tool that seems the most useful, but if possible, use both handouts to conduct two cycles of analysis. Looking at the data from more than one perspective can reveal additional areas of success and needed improvement.

Review the handouts. Handout 13.2A is organized around the data sources that provide evidence about student learning. Handout 13.2B is organized around the learning outcomes for the lesson. You may decide to assign small groups to examine different pieces of data, or you may choose to look at all of the data together. In either case, after investigating each source of data, discuss what it indicates about student learning and understanding. Use the handouts to record notes from your analyses and discussions.

List the data sources in the appropriate boxes on Handout 13.2A Analyzing the Evidence: Data Sources. You identified these sources in the plan for the prototype lesson. Be sure to include any additional sources of data as well.

Discuss and record your ideas about the following items in the appropriate boxes.

- Describe the data that was collected.
- What evidence is there of student understanding?
- What evidence is there of student misunderstanding?
- What is the evidence that the launch of the lesson provided adequate support for students to begin working on the problem(s)?
- What is the evidence that the lesson was adequately scaffolded for all students?

List the learning outcomes for the lesson in the appropriate boxes of the Learning Outcomes section on Handout 13.2B Analyzing the Evidence: Learning Outcomes and Goals.

Discuss and record your reactions to the following prompts in the appropriate boxes.

- What evidence is there that students met the expected outcomes of the lesson?
- What does the evidence tell you about how many achieved the learning outcomes? Can you tell how many students met the outcomes? How many students are close to achieving the outcomes? How many students still need a lot of work to meet the outcomes?
- Looking more closely at students who have met the outcomes, what evidence do you have about why they were successful?
- Looking more closely at students who are near meeting the outcomes, what evidence do you have to indicate what prevented them from meeting the outcomes? What types of instructional experiences might bring them closer to reaching the learning outcomes?
- Looking more closely at students who are still far from meeting the outcomes, what evidence do you have to indicate what prevented them from meeting the outcomes? What types of instructional experiences might bring them closer to reaching the learning outcomes?
- Were there any manipulatives, visuals, or organizers that might have helped or hindered students? What evidence supports this conclusion?
- How might you revise the design of the lesson to help students more effectively reach the learning outcomes? Record some ideas to use in the next session.

List the unit goals for the lesson in the appropriate boxes of the Unit Goals section on Handout 13.2B Analyzing the Evidence: Learning Outcomes and Goals.

Discuss and record your reactions to the following prompts in the appropriate boxes.

- What evidence is there that students have made progress toward the goals of the unit?

- What aspects of the lesson do you think contributed to students' progress toward the goals? What evidence supports this conclusion?

- What aspects of the lesson *did not* contribute to students' progress toward the unit goals? What evidence supports this conclusion?

- Based on the evidence of student learning discussed and the sequence of the unit, what would the next lesson in the unit look like? What would be the expected outcomes? What types of learning activities would you include? How would you meet the needs of students who show readiness for more challenging tasks? What supports would you provide to students who were struggling?

Activity 13.3 Review and Preview

5 minutes

Reviewing Today's Session

The key ideas for this session are

- Using multiple sources of data provides a reliable way to assess student learning.

- Collecting and examining data on student learning can inform teachers of the effectiveness of a lesson.

Previewing the Next Session

In the next session, you will focus on revising the lesson and reflecting on your work. It will be the last session for the group, and your group will use the data from this session (Session 13) to revise your prototype lesson and reflect on what you learned from your work together.

Handout 13.2A
Analyzing the Evidence: Data Sources

Data Source:	
Evidence of Student Learning	**Evidence of Misunderstanding**

Data Source:	
Evidence of Student Learning	**Evidence of Misunderstanding**

Data Source:	
Evidence of Student Learning	**Evidence of Misunderstanding**

Handout 13.2B
Analyzing the Evidence: Learning Outcomes and Goals

Learning Outcomes

Learning Outcome:	
Evidence of Student Learning	Evidence of Misunderstanding

Learning Outcome:	
Evidence of Student Learning	Evidence of Misunderstanding

Unit Goals

Unit Goal:	
Evidence of Progress	**Evidence of Lack of Progress**

Unit Goal:	
Evidence of Progress	**Evidence of Lack of Progress**

Session 14

Reflecting On and Revising the Prototype Lesson

Overview

After analyzing the evidence of student learning and misunderstanding, what aspects of our prototype lesson plan will be revised?

Description

The final stage of the *Teaching by Design* process is revising the collaboratively designed prototype lesson, reflecting on the experience as a whole, and documenting your learning. This process is important because it enables the team to identify the ideas that will inform your mathematics teaching. It is also an opportunity to articulate and share professional knowledge.

Key Ideas

- Revising a lesson plan allows teachers to apply what they learned as a result of teaching the lesson and analyzing evidence of student understanding.
- Reflection is an essential part of professional learning.
- Capturing learning enables teachers to share professional knowledge with others.

Outline of Activities

- 14.1 Revising the Lesson   (60 minutes)
- 14.2 Final Reflections   (30 minutes)

What to Bring

- Copies of the prototype lesson
- Data collected during the teaching of the lesson, which might include students' written work, teachers' observation notes, teachers' reflections, video, and photos of any visual displays
- Handouts from previous session (13.2A and 13.2B)

Facilitator Notes   Session 14

Revising and Reflecting

If this is your first time facilitating the group, please refer to the more detailed facilitator guidelines in the Introduction. As the facilitator, it is generally your job to keep the conversation flowing and watch the clock. Use your judgment to decide when it's appropriate to extend a session for good conversation or when it's time to move on to the next activity. Remember to keep the group norms posted and revise them, as a group, as necessary.

Before the Session

- Make copies of the following handouts for each team member:
    - ☐ 14.1 Revising the Lesson
    - ☐ 14.2 *Teaching by Design* Reflection
- Gather the following materials to be used in this session:
    - ☐ Group norms (from Activity 1.4)
    - ☐ Chart paper
    - ☐ Markers
- Remind team members to bring the following items from previous sessions:
    - ☐ Journal (and writing instruments)
    - ☐ Copies of the prototype lesson
    - ☐ Data collected during the lesson
    - ☐ Handouts 13.2A and 13.2B

During the Session

- Post group norms, and revise as a group as necessary.
- Activity 14.1: help group navigate challenges, serve as recorder, and coordinate additional teaching or meetings.

After the Session

- Remind group of decisions to reteach or additional meetings scheduled.

Activity 14.1 Revising the Lesson

60 minutes

Handout 13.2A Analyzing the Evidence: Data Sources
Handout 13.2B Analyzing the Evidence: Learning Outcomes and Goals
Handout 14.1 Revising the Lesson
Copies of the prototype lesson
Data collected during the lesson

The purpose of developing the lesson in *Teaching by Design,* as explained in Session 12, is not to create a perfect lesson, but to have the experience of drawing on the group's shared expertise to craft a lesson that considers long- and short-term goals, important mathematical ideas, and appropriate instructional practices—all matched with the needs of students. This session will give you the opportunity to reflect on the degree to which your planning has been matched with the needs of the students and to make changes in your lesson so that you might better meet their needs in the future.

In the previous session, your group examined evidence of student learning from a variety of data sources. In this session, you will connect the evidence of student learning with the instructional activities in the lesson and make decisions about how to revise the lesson. Even a lesson that has gone well should be revised based on the data collected during the teaching of that lesson.

Identifying Components for Revision

Review Handouts 13.2A and 13.2B and any notes you took during Session 13. Look at the portions of the handouts that outline the evidence of student learning and misunderstanding.

Read Handout 14.1 and write your ideas on the chart. Your analysis and discussion from Session 13 should help you address the questions on the handout:

- What aspects of the lesson contributed to student learning and should remain in the lesson?
- How can the lesson be revised to more effectively help students achieve the expected outcomes and goals of the lesson?

Share your responses with the group and record the group's responses on chart paper.

Addressing Challenges in Revision

Groups may encounter a variety of challenges as they consider how to revise a lesson. Is your group struggling with any of the following?

Our group members can't agree on how to change the plan. Sometimes group members may have two or more different ideas for how to proceed. Sometimes the solution to this issue is to develop different versions of the lesson. If the revised lesson will be taught and observed, it may be helpful to leave the final decision up to the team member who will be teaching the lesson rather than developing multiple versions. Keep in mind that the revised version of the lesson, like any prototype lesson, is not set in stone. When teachers use the lesson in their classrooms, they will need to make adaptations to the plan.

Discuss how developing and teaching two different versions of the lesson plan might help or hinder the learning experience for the group. What are some drawbacks to having two different plans? Would group members feel safe to share the evidence of student learning for "their" plans?

Our lesson was horrible. We want to rewrite the whole thing. Sometimes a lesson does not go as planned. Improving the lesson often does not require a totally new plan. Consider making minor, but careful, revisions before teaching it again. Perhaps the group miscalculated students' prior knowledge and skills or the task did not motivate students. This is a great learning opportunity. Again, the purpose of developing the prototype lesson in *Teaching by Design* is not to create a perfect lesson, but to have the experience of drawing on the group's shared expertise to craft a lesson that considers long- and short-term goals, important mathematical ideas, and appropriate instructional practices—all matched with the needs of students.

Discuss areas of the lesson where there is evidence of student learning. You might consider keeping these aspects of the lesson. Where did students struggle? How might the task be reworked, questions rephrased, the use of manipulatives either included or removed, or visual materials adapted to better help students achieve the goals of the lesson?

The lesson is too hard. Many students didn't get it. We need to make the lesson easier. Often in this type of professional learning experience, we err on the side of developing a lesson where all students experience immediate success. As a result, the lesson loses its rigor and fails to address important mathematical concepts. In other cases, we develop lessons which are so challenging that no students can reach the goals we have for them. This may be because we have not considered the necessary prerequisite knowledge and skills students need to accomplish the tasks we assign, or because we have expected them to learn too much too quickly. In these cases, it is important to consider whether the confusion students experience will help them learn in the long run, or whether it will interfere with their learning in the future. There may be occasions when it is desirable for students to experience confusion and a sense of disequilibrium. The lesson will never be perfect. What did not work informs what you will do the next day—consolidation of learning is important. The key is that you are not only aware of potential challenges or difficult concepts, but also have planned for them by identifying broad unit goals and what each lesson in the unit will address.

Discuss when it may be desirable for students to be confused and experience disequilibrium. What are the benefits of confusion? What are some of the challenges in having students work past their confusion?

The lesson was great! We don't need to make any changes. Sometimes all students are on task during a lesson, and it may appear that there aren't any changes that need to be made. Other times, comments and data analysis may only focus on the positive, for fear of hurting the group member's feelings if any questions are raised about the lesson. It's important for teams to look closely at all of the evidence of student learning when deciding on the success of a lesson.

Discuss whether or not all of the students showed evidence of learning. How might students be further challenged? Was the lesson rigorous enough? Are there additional supports that might be added for students with special needs?

Making Lesson Changes

Review what the group listed on the chart paper and Handout 14.1. Discuss and decide on the changes you will make in the revised version of the lesson.

Documenting Changes

You and your group are now ready to document changes to your lesson plan. It is important to keep a copy of your original plan. If you are using a computer, be sure to save the revised lesson as another document file. It is also important to be able to compare the first and second versions of the lesson. This comparison can take place when the team discusses the results of the reteaching.

Reteaching the Lesson

You and your group members will probably want to teach the revised lesson in a class that did not experience the first version. Benefits to teaching the revised lesson include the following characteristics:

- The revised lesson uses classroom data to inform the development of the lesson.
- Another opportunity to teach or observe the lesson provides you with another learning experience.
- Revising and reteaching the lesson allows your group to investigate different ideas of mathematics instruction.
- Collecting evidence of student learning from the teaching of the second lesson will allow you to make comparisons between the differences in impact on student learning between the two lesson plans.

Discuss whether or not your group will teach the revised lesson. What would you gain from teaching the revised lesson? When could you find time to discuss the results of the revised lesson?

Activity 14.2 Final Reflections

30 minutes | Handout 14.2 *Teaching by Design* Reflection
All handouts, journal entries, and notes from all previous sessions

The process of reflecting on professional development is a key step in ensuring that your experiences lead to learning and change. Reflection enables you to extract knowledge from experiences and frame questions about the assumptions that influence your teaching. Reflection also allows you to identify areas of strength in your knowledge about students, instruction, and mathematics, as well as areas where more learning would be helpful. Reflection is a key to formulating the next steps in your professional growth.

Review the expected outcomes described at the beginning of this volume and reproduced as follows.

> ### Expected Outcomes for *Teaching by Design in Elementary Mathematics*
>
> - Teachers will deepen their content knowledge for important mathematical concepts in their grade.
> - Teachers will increase their understanding of how students learn these mathematical ideas.
> - Teachers will use their knowledge to develop effective lessons and improve instruction.
> - Teachers will enhance their collaboration skills.

Collect your thoughts about these outcomes on Handout 14.2.

Record your reactions to the following questions in your journal:

- In what ways did you deepen your content knowledge for number and operation concepts described in the Common Core State Standards for fourth and fifth grade?
- What did you learn about how students learn these mathematical ideas?
- How did you use this knowledge in the development of a lesson plan?
- In what ways did you enhance your collaboration with your colleagues?

References and Resources

Stepanek, J., Appel, G., Leong, M., Mangan, M. T., & Mitchell, M. (2007). *Leading lesson study: A practical guide for teachers and facilitators.* Thousand Oaks, CA: Corwin.

Handout 14.1
Revising the Lesson

What aspects of the lesson contributed to student learning and should remain in the lesson?	How can the lesson be revised to more effectively help students achieve the expected outcomes and goals of the lesson?

Handout 14.2
Teaching by Design Reflection

To what extent did you achieve the expected outcomes for *Teaching by Design in Elementary Mathematics?*

- Teachers will deepen their content knowledge for important mathematical concepts in their grade.

- Teachers will increase their understanding of how students learn these mathematical ideas.

- Teachers will use their knowledge to develop effective lessons and improve instruction.

- Teachers will enhance their collaboration skills.

Successes: What worked? What helped produce positive outcomes?

Challenges: What didn't work? In hindsight, what would I/we have changed?

Next steps: Do we want to continue? What should we focus on next?

Index

CORWIN

A SAGE Company

The Corwin logo—a raven striding across an open book—represents the union of courage and learning. Corwin is committed to improving education for all learners by publishing books and other professionaldevelopment resources for those serving the field of PreK–12 education. By providing practical, hands-on materials, Corwin continues to carry out the promise of its motto: **"Helping Educators Do Their Work Better."**

education northwest

CREATING STRONG
SCHOOLS & COMMUNITIES

Education Northwest, formerly known as the Northwest Regional Educational Laboratory, is a nonprofit organization dedicated to transforming teaching and learning. We work with educators, administrators, policymakers, and communities across the country. Headquartered in Portland, Oregon, our mission is to improve learning by building capacity in schools, families, and communities through applied research and development. More information about Education Northwest is available at educationnorthwest.org.

In compliance with GPSR, should you have any concerns about the safety of this product, please advise: International Associates Auditing & Certification Limited The Black Church, St Mary's Place, Dublin 7, D07 P4AX Ireland EUAR@ie.ia-net.com

www.ingramcontent.com/pod-product-compliance
Lightning Source LLC
Chambersburg PA
CBHW080246030426
42334CB00023BA/2718